THE AFRICAN EXPERIENCE
Volume IIIB:
Guide to Resources

THE
AFRICAN
EXPERIENCE

Volume IIIB:
Guide to Resources

edited by
JOHN N. PADEN
and
EDWARD W. SOJA

Northwestern University Press
Evanston 1970

Library of Congress Catalog Card Number: 70-98466
ISBN 0-8101-0316-8
Copyright © 1970 by Northwestern University Press

Book design by Elizabeth G. Stout
Cover design by Edward Hughes
Photograph by Russell Kay
Chi-wara antelope headdress,
used by Bambara (Mali) dance society,
from the collection of Robert Plant Armstrong.

Contents

723175

Introduction

RECOGNIZING THE NEED for more specialized information regarding available materials for courses in African studies, we have decided to supplement the *Bibliography* with this *Guide to Resources.* This guide contains six articles focusing on specific aspects of Africana resources which hopefully can aid the teacher, student, and librarian in the enrichment of course materials and in the development of more comprehensive library collections in African studies.

The first article, by Hans Panofsky, discusses the general availability of reference sources in African studies. It includes reference-filled overviews of the organization and use of Africana resources, directories and personalia, major bibliographic sources, thematic and subject bibliographies, national bibliographies on African countries, reference retrieval projects, and the future of Africana library facilities.

The second article, by Robert Plant Armstrong, talks about developments in African publishing, including the goals of publishing in Africa, the physical and technical aspects of book-manufacturing, the rapidly rising demand for textbooks, and the opportunities for cooperation between publishing companies in Africa and those overseas. The situation in Nigeria, because of its size, impact, and well-established creative and technological base, is given special attention.

In the third article, Hans Panofsky and Robert Koester discuss African journals and newspapers. After a brief historical overview, there is a listing of major African journals arranged into several categories: general journals on Africa, journals specifically related to the *Syllabus* modules, and journals arranged by country. Each entry is briefly annotated to outline its major emphasis, and information is supplied on initial date, frequency, and place of publication. Finally, a short list of African newspapers is included.

African-language publications provide the subject for the fourth article, written by Ahmad Getso, Morris Goodman, Joseph Mabwa, and John Paden. The potential for African language and literature studies at the college level is assessed, and annotated references are given to Hausa and Swahili publications to illustrate the range of literature available in African languages. All titles are translated, annotated, and arranged in five substantive categories: society and culture, history, social change, politics, and literature.

The fifth article, by William Byrne, discusses the range of existing audiovisual aids and explores some of the future techniques which may be available to college teachers in African studies—such as EVR cassettes and videotape for classroom use. A list of nearly 200 audiovisual materials arranged by module topic is included.

The final article elaborates upon the uses of computers in compiling Africana bibliographies, a topic introduced briefly in the first article by Panofsky. Written by Kenneth E. Larimore and Donald Dillaman, it includes a summary of the advantages of using computer technology for reference storage and retrieval, a discussion of the techniques used in generating the *Bibliography,* and a review of the technical aspects of computerized bibliographies in general.

All six articles are intended to provide the student, the teacher, and the librarian with a clear overview of the types of resources which are available or are becoming available in the field of African Studies. In most cases, they are intended to be illustrative rather than comprehensive and, like all the materials of *The African Experience,* are designed not only to inform but to provide suggestions and guidelines for exploring the rich and growing literature on Africa.

J.N.P.
E.W.S.

THE AFRICAN EXPERIENCE
Volume IIIB:
Guide to Resources

Reference Sources
for African Studies

HANS E. PANOFSKY

A COMMENTARY TO A BIBLIOGRAPHY should be a clarification of the nature and the extent of the material under examination; beyond that it should offer additional bibliographic aid as a guide to further research and to provide an overview of the total field of studies. In this essay I propose to coordinate various bibliographic listings and to offer as a further tool a guide to subject and area bibliographies. I will also note briefly the major collections of Africana in this country and abroad. Hopefully the users of *The African Experience* materials will look upon this bibliographic volume not as an appendix to a course, but rather as an essential aid in building a knowledge of the extensive literature on Africa and in indicating the availability of information on each topic.

The contents of the *Bibliography* have been selected with the idea of providing an introduction to the various aspects of African studies, and also a guide for more detailed research. In order to be able to handle with confidence this rich fare one must become aware of the overall resources in the field of Africana, of the organization of these materials, and of the bibliographic aids available to the students and researchers.

THE NATURE AND ORGANIZATION OF AFRICANA

Almost every bibliographic collection of Africana has started as an offshoot of limited and special pursuits—for example, as a repository of mission and travel literature. Increasingly, however, these nuclear collections have lost their specificity and become data sources for cooperative academic activity grouped around issues or sets of problems, while continuing to serve the more traditional self-contained activities of individual scholars. The trend of today's scholarly research on Africa has been to rely more and more on information generated in Africa; and collections have tended to become bodies of material *from* Africa even more than *about* Africa. This has brought about the characteristic and problematic feature of the acquisition and organization of primary material and of statistical, demographic, political, and oral data.

This organization problem is particularly acute for unique material; it is a hard task to collect any body of literature from such a vast and bibliographically unexplored area as Africa where, until relatively recently, publishing, the book trade, and national libraries were practically nonexistent as organized structures. In spite of the difficulties, the last two decades have witnessed a significant level of organization and cooperation which has brought much of the unique material within reach of widely dispersed Africanist scholars. Still, a very great deal remains to be done in order to avoid duplication of efforts and to achieve full bibliographic coordination and dissemination.

Organization of Africana at the national level has been envisioned but not yet attained. It would be an invaluable help to the scholars of all disciplines and would make possible the flourishing of comparative studies which have hitherto been impossible for lack of reliable and controlled data. The bulk of the major collections consists of monographs and secondary sources which can be roughly divided into retrospective and current. Retrospective sources are generally those which are out of print and are available solely through antiquarian dealers or via interlibrary loans. Current sources are those which are available through normal commercial channels. Periodical literature and newspapers may fall into either category, but where the content has not been satisfactorily analyzed a major problem exists in evaluation and distribution of these resources.

The storage of this rapidly expanding body of material and its bibliographic control and retrieval is taxing many a library system. The predicament of libraries reflects a shift in knowledge organization—that is, an increasing departure from disciplinary compartmentalization toward a concentration of resources by research problems. In this process inroads are being made into and across different academic fields.

DIRECTORIES AND PERSONALIA

Turning for a moment from the body of literature about Africa to the body of scholars and specialists producing it, one is struck by the great variety of people, all over the world, directly concerned with the production of information about Africa. It is interesting to note that, in the past, records and data from Africa were not the products of scholars but were the works of civil servants, government officials, traders, educators, keepers of oral tradition, and the like. It is difficult to gather much information about such authors; in fact, anonymity is the rule for most of them, especially the civil servants. African politicians, however, who have generated much data on Africa, may be more visible. Some are described in Ronald Segal's *Political Africa* (London: Stevens, 1961), a Who's Who of personalities and parties; and more recently in *The New African* (New York: Putnam, 1967), a guide to contemporary African leaders, compiled by fifty correspondents of Reuters news agency. There exists a *Who's Who in East Africa* (Nairobi: Marco Survey, 1965–66) and one for southern Africa (which is restricted to whites). Well-known African leaders may also have entries in the British *Who's Who;* other notables may be included in *Current Biography* and *Biography Index,* both published in New York by the H. W. Wilson Company.

Two particular listings of scholars who have worked on Africa deserve notice. In 1963 the UNESCO Secretariat prepared a *Directory of Social Scientists* specializing in African studies. Over 2,000 scholars are listed alphabetically, and a subject and geographical index is included. For listings of Americans especially, the UNESCO directory can be supplemented by the *Directory of Foreign Area Fellows, 1952–1963,* issued by the Foreign Area Fellowship Program, and more currently by the *Roster of Fellows* of the African Studies Association, issued annually.

MAJOR BIBLIOGRAPHIC RESOURCES

A student of Africa will certainly collect a number of books in his field, but he will collect as well a very great number of references to publications he does not own, and so he will often want to make use of the library. Increasingly, Africana librarians feel that they should be in a position not only to provide access to all published sources but to know of the location of unpublished ones as well—especially those which can be borrowed on interlibrary loan or through other arrangements, or where a microfilm copy can be obtained. The basic guide to any library is its catalogue, which at present is usually in the form of a card file. The size of a library is not always indicative of the size of its specialized collections; there are some relatively small libraries which have large African holdings. We are fortunate in having a guide to American library and archival collections on Africa: Peter Duignan, *Handbook of American Resources for African Studies*, Hoover Institution Bibliographical Series, no. 29 (Stanford, 1967). Almost one hundred library and manuscript collections and a somewhat larger number of church and missionary libraries or archives are described either by their curators or by Dr. Duignan. Although the amount of information supplied is not always proportional to the importance of the libraries, this handbook does draw attention to the location of widely dispersed collections, many of which contain unique material. With regard to British collections, the Standing Conference on Library Materials in Africa has issued the *SCOLMA Directory of Libraries and Special Collections on Africa*, 2d ed. (London: Crosby Lockwood, 1967). The best existing guide to French institutions is a series of articles by Joanne Coyle Dauphin in the *African Studies Bulletin*, "French Provincial Centers of Documentation and Research in Africa" (December, 1966), pp. 48–65, with other articles still to appear. With regard to Africana in African countries, a useful though not necessarily complete listing is that compiled by E. W. Dadzie and J. J. Strickland, *Directory of Archives, Libraries and Schools of Librarianship in Africa* (Paris: UNESCO, 1965). We shall soon be able to turn to what is likely to become a definitive and authoritative new guide: Morris Rieger, *Guide to Archival and Manuscript Resources Relating to Africa in the United States*. It will provide comprehensive coverage of the Africa-related archives of American government agencies, the collections of commercial concerns, private papers, and religious and missionary repositories.

A brief description of some of the more important libraries in the United States with major Africana collections may be useful at this point. Not surprisingly, the Library of Congress (L.C.) must be mentioned first. By general agreement, L.C. has more of most things, including Africana; and, consistent with normal library practice, the material on Africa is dispersed according to subject matter. Some of the highlights of L.C.'s material on Africa are listed by Helen Conover in Duignan's *Handbook*, pages 40–51. Harvard University's Widener Library may well rank next in importance for Africana. One may consult the published computer print-out of the shelflist section pertaining to Africa. Books are arranged alphabetically, chronologically, and according to geographical classification. Another library at Harvard, the Peabody Museum of Archaeology and Ethnology, has published an important catalogue. This is an author and subject catalogue, reproduced from catalogue cards, and comprises fifty-five large volumes.

The New York Public Library is virtually a second national library and has great strength in Africana; particularly good are its North African holdings and official documents from all over the continent. Also well known is the Schomburg Collection of Negro History and Literature, administered as a branch of the New York Public Library. About half the volumes in the Schomburg Collection pertain to Africa. The nine-volume catalogue was published in 1962 by the G. K. Hall Company, and the first, two-volume supplement has already appeared.

Among other important collections on Africa in the United States are the libraries at Boston University; the University of California at Los Angeles; Howard University; Northwestern University; and Stanford University, including the Hoover Institution. The Boston University catalogue of *African Government Documents* has been published in a second edition. Howard University has published *A Catalogue of the African Collection in the Moorland Foundation* (1958). The Africana section of Northwestern University Library had its author and title catalogue published in 1962 by G. K. Hall. Since that date it has issued six times a year the *Joint Acquisition List of Africana* which enters alphabetically the Africana acquired by major research libraries in the United States.

Since 1962, American publications on Africa have been listed annually in *U.S. and Canadian Publications on Africa*. This work is issued by the Hoover Institution at Stanford University. The 1965 issue contains around 2,000 items arranged by topics and area, and includes an author index. A similar endeavor is that of the African Bibliographic Center in Washington, D.C., which issues a series of bibliographies, the most useful being *A Current Bibliography on African Affairs*, published monthly by Greenwood Periodicals, Inc., in New York City. An important aspect of these two bibliographies is their indexing of chapters in the increasing number of anthologies that are being published.

Among libraries overseas, particular mention must be made of the University of London's School of Oriental and African Studies and that of the Colonial Office. Catalogues for both these institutions have been published by G. K. Hall. African libraries, except those in the Republic of South Africa, remain quite small. In recent years, however, great efforts have been made by many libraries to collect publications pertaining to their own countries.

THEMATIC AND SUBJECT BIBLIOGRAPHIES

Having mentioned some of the more important libraries on Africana, it is necessary to provide an evaluation of the bibliographic aid now existing for Africana. Perhaps the best place to begin is with the numerous guides which reflect the various approaches to classifying Africana. There are several guides reflecting the different approaches: these are usually ordered by subject and by country, and within these are numerous specialized bibliographies. First of all, a general guide that cannot be too strongly recommended is Helen Conover, *Africa, South of the Sahara: A Selected Annotated List of Writings* (Washington: Government Printing Office, 1963). Over 2,000 items—books, journal articles, and government reports—are arranged geographically in this volume; and an author, title, and subject index are included. The fact that this work does not include works published since 1963 does, of course, detract from its value. Those who are overwhelmed by the size of Miss Conover's selection may wish to consult Kenneth M. Glazier, *Africa, South of the Sahara: A Select and Annotated Bibliography, 1964-1968*, Hoover Institution Bibliographical Series (Stanford, 1969). This list contains a limited number of annotated titles with quotations from, and references to, book reviews; it is limited to books published in English.

Specialized Africana bibliographies exist in most of the academic disciplines. With regard to geography, Richard E. Dahlberg and Benjamin E. Thomas, "Map Resources on Africa," *African Studies Bulletin* (March, 1962), pp. 1-8, is useful, as is their "An Analysis and Bibliography of Recent African Atlases," *African Studies Bulletin* (October, 1962), pp. 23–33. The monthly *Current Geographical Publications*, published by the American Geographical Society, should also be mentioned. This periodical, an up-to-date listing of additions to the large American Geographical Society library collection, arranges recently published materials by topic and region, and includes several sections on Africa.

With regard to archaeology and prehistory the very impressive *Atlas of African Prehistory,* compiled by J. Desmond Clark, was published by the University of Chicago Press in 1967. This pioneer work of scholarship will help to relate human evolution to its natural setting in prehistoric Africa. Those who need a more detailed bibliographic survey on prehistory should consult the Council for Old World Archeology (COWA) Survey published in Cambridge, Massachusetts. Areas nine through fourteen in this survey cover different parts of Africa.

For guides to the growing historical literature on Africa one can recommend strongly the *Journal of African History,* published by Cambridge University Press, which appeared three times a year from 1960 to 1968 and four times a year since then. This journal includes discussions of new findings as well as reinterpretations of old ones. The book reviews are of a higher standard than those of most other journals. For an overview of the field of African history see Philip Curtin, *African History* (New York: Macmillan, 1964). This is a brief bibliographical essay of fifty-five pages. Those who require a strict bibliography may wish to consult Vernon MacKay's chapter in *Guide to Historical Literature* (American Historical Association, 1961), pp. 745-69. An increasing amount of African history is also to be found in the quarterly *Historical Abstracts* (Santa Barbara, Calif.) and the annual *International Bibliography of Historical Sciences,* published by Oxford University Press.

African studies was the major preserve of anthropology until about the 1940s, and so it is not suprising that the anthropological literature is relatively well indexed and even abstracted. This is largely the work of the International African Institute, a membership organization founded in London in 1928. The Institute produces the quarterly journal *Africa,* largely anthropological and linguistic in coverage. Each issue includes a lengthy bibliography on Africa classified into broad thematic categories. Since 1950 the Institute has also published the quarterly *African Abstract* which includes abstracts, arranged geographically, of the more important articles already listed in *Africa.* There is an annual index, arranged by author, ethnic group, and subject. The Institute has published a part of its catalogue in book form. To date, volumes on the ethnology, sociology, and linguistics of West Africa, Northeast Africa, East Africa, and Southeast-Central Africa and Madagascar have appeared. Within each volume the entries are arranged by country and tribe, with ethnological entries being separated from linguistic entries. A concise base-line study pertaining to particular ethnic groups is found in the Institute's "Ethnographic Survey of Africa." These brief case studies of approximately one hundred pages each have been appearing since 1950. Quite recently, Gordon D. Gibson has compiled "A Bibliography of Anthropological Bibliographies: Africa" in *Current Anthropology* (December, 1969, pp. 527-66).

A reference has already been made to linguistics in connection with anthropology. Increasingly, however, the former is treated as a separate discipline. The annual *Bibliographie linguistique* (Utrecht: Spectrum) is important in this field. The *Handbook of African Languages* (International African Institute) with its several issues written by various authors—particularly A. N. Tucker and Malcolm Guthrie—contains numerous bibliographical references. The *Handbook* is an attempt to list and classify African languages.

Resources pertaining to political science are poorly served bibliographically. A useful general bibliography is the *International Bibliography of Political Science,* one of a series issued by the International Committee for Social Science Documentation. (Others in this series include *Sociology, Economics,* and *Social and Cultural Anthropology.*) The *Bulletin of the Public Affairs Information Service,* usually cited as PAIS, tends to be more up to date than the *International Bibliographies.* Brode, John. *The Process of Modernization* an annotated bibliography on the sociocultural aspects of development (Cambridge, Mass.: Harvard University Press, 1969). The African Section of the Library of Congress has prepared guides to official publications of former British East Africa, French Equatorial Africa, French West Africa, the Rhodesias and Nyasaland, Sierra Leone and Gambia, Madagascar, Ghana, and Nigeria. For Nigeria, in fact, the guide was initially issued in 1959 and revised in 1966. These guides, however, frequently list only official government publications.

A useful index to the periodical literture has been prepared by William John and Judith L. Hanna, *Politics in Black Africa* (East Lansing, Michigan: Michigan State University, 1964).

To keep up to date with African political happenings one may recommend strongly Colin Legum and John Drysdale, *African Contemporary Record, Annual Survey and Documents, 1968-1969* (London: Africa Research Limited), and the two loose-leaf services offered by the same publisher. In recent years the African coverage of *The Times* (London), *le Monde* (Paris), and *The New York Times* has been improving. Important political and economic events have been usefully summarized, usually two months after their occurrence, in the "News in Brief" section of *Africa Report* (Washington, D.C.). This section was discontinued in late 1969, but the format of *Africa Report* has been revised to incorporate news of recent events from associated reporters in the field. A publicly available source on foreign radio broadcasts and newspapers is the translations in the Central Intelligence Agency's *Foreign Broadcast Information Service & Daily Report on Africa* (U.S. Department of Commerce, Joint Publications Research Service).

The importance of African newspapers for an understanding of that continent cannot be exaggerated. The more prominent newspapers, at least from the point of view of the advertisers, are listed in the *Advertising and Press Annual of Africa*. Those held by American libraries are listed, although rather poorly, in the Library of Congress, *African Newspapers in Selected American Libraries,* 3rd ed. (Washington, D.C.: Government Printing Office, 1965). Readers wanting to locate negative microfilm must consult *Newspapers on Microfilm*, 6th ed. (Library of Congress, 1967). Some ten African newspaper titles are currently being microfilmed by the Library of Congress, and prints are widely distributed in this country. Other titles are filmed by the Foreign Newspaper Projects and are available from the Center for Research Libraries in Chicago. (Further discussion of African newspapers is contained in the article by Panofsky and Koester, pp. 31–51 below.)

Bibliographical work on economics, insofar as it pertains to Africa, has largely been accomplished by the Library of the United Nations Economic Commission for Africa (ECA) in Addis Ababa, Ethiopia. It issues accession lists and guides to statistical publications. Also useful is the publication by the Commission for Technical Cooperation in Africa South of the Sahara (CCTA), now merged with the Organization of African Unity (OAU), *Inventory of Economic Studies Concerning Africa South of the Sahara* (ca. 1960), and its supplement.

With reference to agriculture, a model for amount and detail of coverage is the Library of Congress, *Agricultural Development Schemes in Sub-Saharan Africa* (1963), compiled by Ruth S. Freitag. This bibliography contains 1,783 well-indexed entries.

Labor in Africa has been well documented bibliographically. William H. Friedland has compiled *Union, Labor and Industrial Relations* (Cornell University, Center for International Studies, 1965), an annotated bibliography listing 683 items alphabetically by author and with a subject and area index. The United States Bureau of Labor Statistics *Bulletin,* no. 1473, is a "Bibliography on Labor in Africa, 1960–1964." Migratory labor in sub-Saharan Africa has been the subject of much study. The present writer compiled a bibliography in 1961 which was published by the Commission for Technical Cooperation in Africa, South of the Sahara (CCTA publication no. 79, 1961, Section IV). Unfortunately the CCTA's Inter-African Labor Institute *Bulletin* ceased to appear with the May, 1965, issue. A more recent contribution is *Manpower and Unemployment Research in Africa,* a newsletter published by the Centre for Developing-Area Studies, McGill University, containing much useful bibliographic information.

Sociological research has only recently been undertaken in Africa. A useful bibliography is the one compiled by the Department of Social Anthropology, University of Edinburgh, *African Urbanization* (London: International African Institute, 1965), a reading list of selected books, articles, and reports. To keep up to date in the field of urban studies as it pertains to Africa one should regularly examine *African Urban Notes*, a research newsletter which has been issued periodically since 1966. Use of newsletters as a means of noting new publications and current research is likely to spread to other disciplines. A very useful listing of censuses is to be found in Texas University Population Research Center, *International Census Bibliography: Africa* (Austin, Texas: Bureau of Business Research, 1965), which can be supplemented by the *Population Index* issued by the Office of Population Research at Princeton.

Readers of psychology will find a useful reference source in *Psychological Abstracts* issued by the American Psychological Association in Lancaster, Pennsylvania, and more specifically from E. L. Klingelhofer, *A Bibliography of Psychological Research and Writing in Africa* (Uppsala: Scandinavian Institute of African Studies, 1967). Those who require more detail in the field of aptitude measurement and testing may use L. E. Andor, *Aptitude and Abilities of the Black Man in Sub-Saharan Africa, 1784–1963* (Johannesburg: South African Council for Scientific and Industrial Research, 1966).

Law has its *Journal of African Law,* and there is a Center of African Law at Columbia University, which publishes a digest of African law as well as a newsletter. We may expect a great bibliographical output once the new law center being developed in Addis Ababa is fully established.

For sources on education in Africa there are a number of fairly helpful bibliographies. Especially important is John W. Hanson and Geoffrey W. Gibson, *African Education and Development Since 1960* (Michigan State University, 1966), which summarizes all major studies through 1965 with compact annotations and evaluations. Cole S. Brembeck and John P. Keith, *Education in Emerging Africa* (Michigan State University, 1963) is a select annotated bibliography. Those who want to investigate education in more depth can be referred to the University of London Institute of Education, *Catalogue of the Collection of Education in Tropical Areas* (London: G. K. Hall, 1964); this appears in three volumes—author, regional, and subject indexes.

Finally we turn to the humanities. So far as African literature is concerned, we have the large bibliography of Janheinz Jahn, *A Bibliography of Neo-African Literature* (New York: Praeger, 1965); also, Barbara Abrash, *Black African Literature in English Since 1952, Works and Criticism* (New York: Johnson Reprint Corporation, 1967); the more modest effort of Margaret Amosu, *A Preliminary Bibliography of Creative African Writing in European Languages* (University of Ibadan, 1963); and J. A. Ramsaran, *New Approaches to African Literature* (Ibadan: Ibadan University Press, 1965). A useful, although somewhat dated, publication is the special issue on the arts issued by the African Studies Association in May, 1962. Two recent bibliographies compiled by L. J. P. Gaskin in 1965, *A Select Bibliography of Music in Africa* and *A Bibliography of African Art,* are very impressive (both published by Oxford University Press for the International African Institute).

We are poorly equipped with bibliographies concerning anything but material in the printed medium. With regard to film we have the recent UNESCO

Catalogue selectif international de films ethnographiques sur l'Afrique noire (Paris: UNESCO, 1967) and the much more modest African Studies Association Committee of Fine Arts and Humanities, *African Film Bibliography* (1965). Alan P. Merriam's *African Music on LP: An Annotated Discography* (Evanston, Ill: Northwestern University Press, 1970) provides annotated and cross-indexed listings of all commercial LP recordings of African music released through 1965.

With regard to academic work in progress, one can consult *Africa*, compiled by the United States Department of State, Office of External Research. Useful too is Centre International de Documentation Africaine (CIDESA), *Bulletin of Information on Theses and Studies in Progress or Proposed* (Brussels). Dissertations on Africa completed at United States universities up to 1960/61 are catalogued in *A List of American Doctoral Dissertations on Africa* (Washington, D.C.: Government Printing Office, 1962). This is updated somewhat by Doris M. Cruger, *A List of American Doctoral Dissertations on Africa Covering 1961/62 through 1964/65...*(Ann Arbor, Mich.: University Microfilms, 1967). For French dissertations on Africa, note the compilations by Marion Dinstel: *List of French Dissertations on Africa, 1884–1961* (Boston: G. K. Hall, 1966). Dissertations completed in the British Isles are listed in *United Kingdom Publications and Theses on Africa,* an annual issued by the Standing Committee on Library Materials on Africa (SCOLMA).

BIBLIOGRAPHIES ON AFRICAN COUNTRIES

Most bibliographies of this type are really national listings of publications issued in or about a particular country. Ideally, there should be retrospective bibliographies and current supplements. We have few retrospective ones, however, though several good ones do exist for Ghana (Gold Coast): A. W. Cardinall, *A Bibliography of the Gold Coast,* issued as a companion volume to the Census Report of 1931 (no less than 5,168 items were identified by this amateur bibliographer as having something to do with the Gold Coast) and updated versions of this bibliography by A. F. Johnson, *A Bibliography of Ghana, 1930–1961* (London: Longmans, 1964), and David Brokensha and S. I. A. Kotei, "A Bibliography of Ghana: 1958–1964," *African Studies Bulletin* (September, 1967), pp. 35–79. An annual national bibliography has also begun to appear, starting with 1965, while *Ghana, A Guide to Official Publications, 1872–1968,* compiled by Julian W. Witherell and Sharon Lockwood, is a more recent addition to the long list of official publications issued by the Library of Congress.

No other African country, exluding South Africa, has such complete bibliographic coverage as Ghana, although bibliographies for the Sudan and Mali are good: Richard Leslie Hill, *A Bibliography of the Anglo-Egyptian Sudan from the*

Earliest Times to 1937 (London: Oxford University Press, 1939); Abdel Rahman el Nasri, *A Bibliography of the Sudan, 1938-1958* (London: Oxford University Press, 1962); and Paule Brasseur, *Bibliographie générale du Mali* (Dakar: IFAN, 1964). Other useful national bibliographies are listed in Constance M. Winchell's *Guide to Reference Books,* 8th ed. (Chicago: American Library Association, 1967), pp. 507-12. Also noteworthy are the bibliographies of Malawi (1965, supplement 1969) and Kenya (1967), the first two numbers of the Syracuse University Eastern African Bibliographic Series, which has also issued "occasional bibliographies" in a variety of subject areas for the three East African countries and for Bechuanaland (1966, supplement 1968), Lesotho (1968), and Swaziland (1968). Among current national bibliographies, the only satisfactory one is the annual *Nigerian Publications,* issued since 1950-52 by the Ibadan University Library. Finally, the *African Studies Bulletin* regularly publishes short bibliographies on African countries and certain special topics which are useful.

For the last four years annual compilations have been made of books and journals about Africa published outside that continent. As mentioned above, the Hoover Institution has issued since 1962 a series entitled *United States and Canadian Publications on Africa.* The British publish, through their Standing Conference on Library Materials on Africa, *United Kingdom Publications and Theses on Africa,* and the Germans publish *Afrika: Bibliographie 1960-61* (Bonn: Deutsche Afrika Gesellschaft).

REFERENCE RETRIEVAL PROJECTS

The need for bibliographers and librarians to cope with the rapidly increasing flow of publications has led toward cooperation and mechanization. No one institution alone can meet all the requests made of it. In the United States a number of libraries have formed the Cooperative African Microform Project (CAMP), which is administered by the Center for Research Libraries in Chicago. CAMP holds master negatives of bulky and infrequently used research material and has begun to distribute guides to some of its collections.

The African Studies Association in America has, through its Archives-Libraries Committee, fostered cooperation and helped bring about the establishment of an African Section at the Library of Congress. On an international level too, cooperation has given rise to the Standing Committee of African University Libraries; a series of conferences have also been held, the most ambitious of which was the International Conference on African Bibliography, which hoped to bring order to diverse and duplicate efforts and to bring publications on Africa under bibliographical control. The proceedings and papers of this conference, held in Nairobi in 1967, are about to be published by Frank Cass & Company in London, edited by J. D. Pearson and Ruth Jones.

Various methods have been developed for the automatic retrieval of bibliographic data. Perhaps the most successful of these computer techniques has been called Keyword In Context (KWIC) and the more advanced Keyword Out of Context (KWOC), discussed in more detail elsewhere in this volume. These indexing devices were invented by the late Hans Peter Luhn of the International Business Machines Corporation. They include the arrangement, by computer, of entries according to author and/or by each word of the title, except those which may be specifically excluded. In the case of KWOC, these terms are arranged alphabetically along the left-hand margin. The advantages of this system are that input is relatively inexpensive and that the bibliography can be updated easily. Its disadvantage is that the imprecision of a title may fail to give a proper clue to the subject matter; descriptors or annotations may be added, however, to reduce this problem.

To attain some degree of bibliographical control is obviously a costly matter. But small-scale, amateurish efforts will not suffice to bring order into the mass of publications on Africa. What is needed is a large-scale effort or series of coordinated efforts to analyze and index all publications on and from Africa. This information must be placed into an electronic memory with the ability to reproduce it rapidly, and at a reasonable cost, when and where needed.

So far the most substantial attempts to handle Africana in a new way have been made in France by the Center for Analysis and Documentary Research for Black Africa (CARDAN); René Bureau and Françoise Izard, former directors of CARDAN, describe their work in the *African Studies Bulletin* (December, 1967), pp. 67–81. They have analyzed and abstracted a large amount of periodical literature and have experimented with the development of a standardized language (SYNTOL), thus opening the way to automatic retrieval on a large scale. The Library of Congress and many other libraries in the United States are experimenting along similar and different lines. Before very long, one or more of these centers will not merely analyze the data, but, even more important, will supply the sources on demand.

THE FUTURE OF AFRICANA LIBRARY FACILITIES

This essay has tried to give an overall picture of the field of Africana and to underline the shift in knowledge organization which allows for the concentration of materials from different disciplines or across disciplines within a geographic area — in this case, Africa. The increasing production of, and demand for, primary documentary material in the form of research data, conference papers, political ephemera and official publications, and the like, all require different technical handling if they are to be made available in a significant way. One must realize that no great improvement can be expected in the influx and analysis of Africana without a closer and more rational cooperation between institutions in America and those in Africa, Europe, and elsewhere. Great efforts must converge toward the creation of national bibliographic centers in each country or region of Africa. This cannot be accomplished unless qualified professionals are trained and employed to provide for these basic necessities of scholarship.

2

Developments
in African Publishing

ROBERT PLANT ARMSTRONG

THE RELATIONSHIP BETWEEN PUBLISHING IN AFRICA and university level African studies is direct: the physical facilities, technical and professional skills, and publishing priorities which are being established in Africa at present will affect not only patterns of educational and economic development in Africa but also the opportunity within the new African states for cultural and scientific expression which has too often been stifled in the past for lack of communications media. University-level social sciences, as well as the arts and humanities, are in many ways dependent on the published word: for communication between scholars, for creative expression, for the raw material of research, for reports of research, for the teaching of students. The growth of publishing industries in Africa at present is not, in most cases, being premised on the needs of university "African studies"; yet the net result may be partly to that end. This decade has witnessed the accelerated growth of university presses, large-scale commercial African presses, government printing offices, international subsidiaries, cooperative arrangements with non-African publishing houses, and, perhaps of most importance, small-scale private printing facilities. In this essay I will try to identify the goals of publishing in Africa, discuss Nigeria as a case study, outline certain financial and production aspects of publishing in Africa, and suggest that more creative actions are necessary in terms of cooperative publishing efforts.

THE GOALS OF AFRICAN PUBLISHING

African specialists and statesmen have clearly defined[1] publishing goals for

1. Conference of African States on the Development of Education in Africa, Addis Ababa, May, 1961; Meeting of Experts on the Adaptation of the General Secondary School Curriculum in Africa, Tananarive, July, 1962; Regional Conference on the Planning and Organization of Literacy Programmes in Africa, Abidjan, March, 1964; Conference of African Ministers of Education, Abidjan, March, 1964.

the 34 independent Black African states south of the Sahara.[2] Planners have projected that by 1980 approximately 32.8 million pupils will be in elementary schools, 5.9 million in secondary schools, and 250,000 students in universities.[3] In terms of book needs, these projected enrollments mean that in 1980 more than 13 billion text pages will be required (400 pages per student) for the elementary schools, 6 billion text pages for students in the secondary schools, and 500 million for those in the universities (each of the latter two estimates representing an increment over the basic 400 pages per student). In addition, to support those who have already achieved literacy, an additional 4 billion pages are deemed desirable.[4]

These objectives are modest enough when contrasted with book production in Europe, where the annual per capita book consumption in major publishing countries is 135 times that of Africa.[5] In Europe, 418 titles are published for each million people; in Africa, the figure is six.[6] Africa, with 9.4 per cent of the world's population, publishes only 1.5 per cent of the world's books. Even if the 1980 objectives are reached in Africa, the number of pages of educational book production will have increased from 20 per person per year to only 72, while those of general book production will have risen from 4 to 48 per person per year.

Despite the fact that the proposed level of book production in 1980 will still be relatively low, it will represent a dramatic increase in Africa. Also, if one of the major objectives defined at Addis Ababa in 1961 is fulfilled—the eradication of illiteracy by 1980—this would indicate a highly significant role for book publishers. At present, three out of every four books used in African countries are imported.[7] This clearly constitutes a most unfavorable situation, and there can be little doubt that during the next decade there will be considerable change in this proportion.

The names of publishers currently operating in the 34 sub-Saharan African countries are listed at the end of this essay. Although this list is not wholly reliable, excluding some publishers while perhaps wrongly including others, it is probably the most complete listing available anywhere.

2. Botswana, Burundi, Cameroon, Central African Republic, Chad, Congo (Brazzaville), Democratic Republic of the Congo, Dahomey, Ethiopia, Gabon, Gambia, Ghana, Guinea, Ivory Coast, Kenya, Lesotho, Liberia, Madagascar, Malawi, Mali, Mauritania, Mauitius, Niger, Nigeria, Rwanda, Senegal, Sierra Leone, Somalia, Swaziland, Tanzania (United Republic of), Togo, Uganda, Upper Volta, Zambia (UNESCO, "Report of the Meeting," COM/CS/68/3/7, p. 5 n).

3. *Ibid.,* p. 11. Elsewhere the figure is placed slightly lower.

4. *Ibid.*

5. Based on the statement made by Tor Gjesdal at the opening of the Meeting of Experts on Book Development in Africa (UNESCO, COM/CS/68/3/INF.4, p. 3).

6. *Ibid.*

7. E. Wegman, "Book Development in Africa," *UNESCO Chronicle,* XIV, no. 4, 145-48.

THE EXAMPLE OF NIGERIA

Because of close relationship between publishing and *national* contexts, it may be useful to illustrate the range of publishing facilities within a single country. The publishing industry appears to be more vital in Nigeria than in any other of the countries with which we are here concerned.[8] *Publisher's World* lists 40 publishers in Nigeria; the Franklin Book Programs' report lists 24 more; and I have been able to identify 3 houses which are not listed by either of the above. Even so these inventories do not fully exhaust the list of those entrepreneurs who have, at one time or another, published a book or two. The consideration of such once-in-a-while publishers is important because in Nigeria, in Ghana, and in other African countries, a bookstore owner or a printer has on occasion turned his capital and his interests toward the publication of a book. This phenomenon of the occasional publisher is perhaps nowhere as marked as in Ethiopia, where a business man with no publishing experience may undertake to select, to cause to be manufactured, and subsequently to market a work on the basis of a one-time venture. One suspects, however, that this kind of individual entrepreneur is less likely to be found in Nigeria, and that it is more likely to be the bookstore or print-shop owner who characterizes the Nigerian "occasional" small-scale publishing industry.

The hospitality of Nigeria as a publishing environment has been recognized by Europeans for some years now. Oxford University Press has a quasi-independent editorial and sales operation there (i.e., the Nigerian house may undertake publishing projects), as have Thomas Nelson, Heinemann, and Longman. The only American commercial firm to be represented in Nigeria has been McGraw-Hill, whose agent has subsequently left. It must also be remembered that it was in Nigeria that the first "African" publishing house was started, the African Universities Press, begun in 1962 by André Deutsch and supported by European and Nigerian capital. By "the first 'African' publishing house" is meant the first one staffed with professionals and dedicated to publishing in the same full-time developmental fashion as that which characterizes European and American publishing houses.

For a variety of reasons, Nigeria has been more fortunate than many other African countries. There seems to be a particular genius to her peoples which has provided a viable milieu for books. Further, this genius has been implemented by an intelligent public in whose eyes the ability to be articulate is honored; by a vigorous entrepreneurial tradition; and by a devotion to education and, therefore, to literacy.

This view is supported by the fact that there exist side by side in Nigeria two publishing industries: one imported, publishing and marketing European-type

8. For a fuller treatment of book publishing in Nigeria, see my article, "Book Publishing in Nigeria: Industry with a Future?" *Africa Report,* April, 1966, pp. 56–57.

books in European ways; and the other wholly indigenous. This latter industry has been centered in Onitsha—at least prior to the civil war—and was given over to the publication of short works of fiction and instruction which have been called *chapbooks.* These books are intimately related to their public, as is indicated by their proliferation and their sales. Chapbooks speak directly to their readers in a language they understand and in terms of subjects that are important to them. Further, the fact that they are brief and are often printed in considerable quantity means that they can be sold at prices the public can afford. The success of the chapbook argues for the view that there is a viable book market in Nigeria. The only problem is how to approach it in its own terms, with subject matter, forms, prices, and methods of distribution which are functionally related to the values, the needs, and the wishes of the public. Too often, however, this dynamic publishing area is overlooked and the imported model of European publishing is pursued. Yet it is clear that the Nigerian is going to have a very limited number of his book needs met by European books. Granting that there are unique factors at work in Nigeria—as indeed there are in every country—one may nonetheless point to the larger area of problems that are shared in common by Nigeria and other African countries, and regret that this natural and viable book industry has not been studied for the broader lessons it has to offer. One cannot help but think that such a study, and perhaps even support of these "kitchen" publishers, would be at least as valuable as the importation of numbers of Western publishers who appear to seek to impose upon Nigeria models of their own London and New York publishing values and techniques.

At least one major writer has allied himself to this indigenous publishing industry. Chinua Achebe has had published by Etudo, Ltd. (Onitsha) his short story, *The Sacrificial Egg.* There have been rumors that other established writers have used the chapbook form and market, though not with works as clearly within the international traditions of art-literature as is Achebe's story.

In a sense the Mbari Artists and Writers Club, in its publication program, has represented the topping-off of this indigenous tradition, even though much of its energy and direction derived from the efforts of the imaginative, sympathetic, and energetic European, Mr. Ulli Beier. The Mbari publications—a novel, plays, collections of drawings, books of verse—and the closely allied journal, *Black Orpheus,* have been clearly African. The titles of the Mbari group were written, designed, produced, and marketed in Africa, by and for Africans. Its writers and artists were, and are—for a newly revitalized *Black Orpheus* is now in a second phase of its existence—dedicated to finding and subsequently to practicing their art in clearly African voices.

As Mbari, a formal publishing operation of international repute, stands at the apex of this indigenous structure, so the African Universities Press stands at the apex of the imported tradition. It has become significantly Africanized, and thus is a European publishing structure controlled and executed by Africans. The imported European publishing industry is almost wholly given over to the publishing of schoolbooks, with the exception of certain houses who also publish serious scholarly works addressed to highly informed readers in the interest of furthering specialized professional knowledge and research. This publishing structure is, as I have indicated, comprised of Oxford University Press and the local offices of three other British houses—Heinemann, Longman, and Nelson, all of which have African managers.

Even though European subsidiaries, these houses are contributing to the Nigerianization of the nation's publishing—not only by means of their having engaged Nigerians to manage and run their operations there, but also by Nigerianizing their books. It is a well-known fact that not too many years ago African children learned the geography of Europe at the expense of learning about their own vast lands. This situation now no longer prevails. Further, with such projects as the Ibadan History Series, edited by Professor J. F. Ade Ajayi of the University of Ibadan and published by Longman, there is occurring research into African history that leads directly to the publication of books which will affect the nature of Nigerian publishing as it becomes integrated into, and thus irrevocably a function of, the national culture of Nigeria.

The Nigerian publishing industry rests upon a capable creative and technological base. Its professional base is in the process of being established. As far as its creative base is concerned, there is a solid resource of published writers of poetry, drama, and the novel in Nigeria. Its scholarly writers too are well represented in the lists of Nigerian, European, and American publishers. Writers of textbooks for use in the curricula of the elementary and secondary schools are developing apace, although textbook writing seems to be a specialized skill perfected by Western educationalists and possibly not yet as highly developed a craft in Nigeria as it is in New York and Boston. Further, of course, the writing of textbooks reflects a national policy of education which will become increasingly Nigerianized. Naturally, textbook writers will reflect this, as will the publishing industry. While Franklin was in operation in Nigeria (1964-68), it sponsored workshops in textbook writing which were popular and, according to reports, effective.[9]

At present, book paper is not manufactured in Nigeria, which inevitably means an increase in the ultimate book prices. Similarly, printing equipment must also be imported. It must be noted, however, that in this respect Nigeria is relatively fortunate: there are literally hundreds of small print-shops in the major towns and cities which are capable of producing pamphlets and small

9. Franklin Book Programs, Inc., is a nonprofit American educational organization governed by a board of directors including book publishers, educators, librarians, and others. The program, which operates in new nations around the world, does not itself publish books but rather assists local publishers in training personnel, choosing manuscripts, and assisting with the legal and professional arrangements necessary to book publishing.

books. There are, in addition, aside from the government printer in Lagos, two major printing houses: Caxton in Ibadan, and Gaskiya in Zaria. There is adequate reason to suspect that these two presses alone have the potential capacity to manufacture all the books needed in Nigeria through 1980.

As far as publishing personnel are concerned, there are those among the small printers devoting their resources to the chapbooks who are obtaining valuable publishing experience. Also, of course, those who are being trained in the offices of the European houses will form a rich base for the future of the publishing industry in Nigeria.

At present, however, Nigeria is not self-sufficient. In 1965, the last year for which I have data, Nigeria imported in excess of six million dollars in books and pamphlets; the greatest part of this money was spent with British publishers.

FINANCE, PRODUCTION, AND PERSONNEL ASPECTS OF AFRICAN PUBLISHING

In 1965, the 34 African countries we are concerned with published 1,310 titles—both "books" (over 49 pages) and "pamphlets" (5–48 pages)—for a total number of 7.3 million copies. (See Table 1.) At the same time they imported—chiefly from the United Kingdom (15,326,000) and France (5,850,000)—23,856,100 copies of books and pamphlets. Ninety per cent of these imports in all probability were educational books. These 1965 book imports cost the African countries in excess of $64,000,000, which was the value of British and French books alone.[10] An FAO estimate of $38,100,000 for the year is clearly inadequate. The importance of this money to the development of African publishing industries—and in turn to the African economies—is clear. With a target increase of from 20 (in 1965) to 72 pages per person per year by 1980, it is clear that publishing needs will have nearly quadrupled. It is incumbent upon African publishers, with aid and support from their governments, to take advantage of this growth and to lead the way in the Africanization of letters and of education. Even without the influence of gradual inflation, the cost of English and French book imports would be $256,000,000[11] in 1980, unless there is a significant development in African publishing potential.

10. UNESCO, "Books in the Promotion of Development in Africa," COM/CS/3/5, p. 6 (Meeting of Experts on Book Development in Africa, Accra, February 13–19, 1968).

11. This assumes that the 1965 figure represents the value of the books actually needed, but the chances are that the amount of books bought was below the number needed—thus the figure would be higher, since the base would be greater than $64,000,000.

Tables 1, 2, 3, and 4 provide detailed information on the numbers of books published and the numbers required. In the latter three of these tables, figures are given for "book units," a mythical integer invented by UNESCO's book experts. A "book unit" is simply the sixteen-page signature which is the composite unit of books, since it is "in sixteens" (or multiples thereof) that books are printed. A 192-page book, for example, uses twelve such signatures, or "book units."

TABLE 1
PRODUCTION OF BOOKS
(NUMBER OF TITLES), 1965–66

Country	Year	Books	Pamphlets	Total
Burundi	1966	11	6	17
Cameroon	1966	11	19	30
Central African Rep.	1966	–	10	10
Ethiopia	1962	n.a.	n.a.	178
Gabon	1965	9	1	10
Ghana	1965	49	176	225
Guinea	1966	1	7	8
Ivory Coast	1966	6	–	6
Kenya	1966	125	n.a.	125
Liberia	1966	5	6	11
Madagascar	1966	64	72	136
Malawi	1966	9	5	14
Mauritius	1966	17	23	40
Nigeria	1964	145	13	158
Rwanda	1962	n.a.	n.a.	23
Senegal	1962	n.a.	n.a.	67
Sierra Leone	1966	48	8	56
Somalia	1965	17	–	17
Tanzania[a]	1962	n.a.	n.a.	75
Uganda	1964	65	–	65
Zambia	1965	11	28	39
Total[b]				1,310

SOURCE: UNESCO, "Assessment of Africa's Book Needs," COM/CS/68/3/5 Add., p. 5 (Meeting of Experts on Book Development in Africa, Accra, February 13–19, 1968).

[a] These statistics are for Zanzibar only.
[b] Approximate total, since the figures are for different years.
n.a. not available

With regard to manufacturing, the UNESCO report comments:

Printing facilities do exist in Africa. The Franklin Book Program reports that there is presently no shortage of printing capacity in Africa. That is to say, the experts felt that the *printing plants in existence were adequate for the*

TABLE 2

DEVELOPMENT OF FIRST-LEVEL EDUCATION
AND BOOK NEEDS, 1975–80 (IN THOUSANDS)

	1965 *(base year)[a]*	*1975*	*1980*
Total number of pupils	14,407	25,800	32,808
Minimal number of book-units (25 per pupil)	360,175	645,000	820,200
Total number of teachers	366,774	738,800	937,400
Minimal number of book-units (500 per teacher)	183,387	369,400	468,700
Total number of inspectors	3[b]	5,172	6,600
Minimal number of book-units (900 per inspector)	2,700	4,654	5,940

SOURCE: UNESCO, "Assessment of Africa's Book Needs," COM/CS/68/3/5/ Add., p. 16 (Meeting of Experts on Book Development in Africa, Accra, February 13–19, 1968).
[a] Book stock needs shown in this column *do not* represent book stocks actually existing in 1965, but are merely an indication, for purposes of comparison, of the level of stocks which would have been needed in 1965 according to minimal criteria.
[b] Estimated.

amount of book printing that was being done or was foreseen in the immediate future.[12]

It is generally acknowledged that the large printing plant built by UNESCO at Yaoundé has the capability to provide enough books for a very great area composed of several neighboring nations. Certainly the plants in Ghana and Nigeria can do as well, and the East African Institute Press does admirably by the East African Publishing House. There seems, therefore, some reason for an only-slightly-guarded optimism. When I was in Africa in 1963, both the major plants in Nigeria were dramatically underemployed, and the manufacture of 145 books listed in Table 1 as the total book production of Nigeria for 1965–66 would hardly seem to suggest that their capacities have been strained. (This is all the more true when one realizes that the figure of 145 titles includes the product of other presses as well.)

There are—or were as of 1968—four paper mills in the African states with which we are concerned: in Ethiopia, Congo-Kinshasa, Kenya, and Swaziland. There are definite plans to build ten additional mills in Africa and studies are being made to ascertain the practicability of building a mill in Nigeria.

12. UNESCO, "Books in the Promotion of Development in Africa," p. 14. The italics are mine; the tautology evidenced in this statement is not atypical of the general state of information concerning book publishing in Africa.

TABLE 3

DEVELOPMENT OF SECOND-LEVEL EDUCATION
AND BOOK NEEDS, 1975–80 (IN THOUSANDS)

		1965 (base year)[a]	1965	1980
General Education	Number of pupils	847.30	3,078.9	3,986
	Minimal number of book-units (62 per pupil)	52,536	190,892	247,132
Technical vocational education	Number of pupils	109.5[b]		
	Minimal number of book-units	6,022[b]		
1st state	Number of pupils		667.2	984.2
	Minimal number of book-units (53 per pupil)		35,361	52,162
2d state	Number of pupils		291.4	563.2
	Minimal number of book units (67 per pupil)		19,524	37,734
Regular training	Number of pupils	97.5[b]		
	Minimal number of book-units	8,000		
1st stage	Number of pupils		154.5	93
	Minimal number of book-units (63 per pupil)		9,733	5,859
2d stage	Number of pupils		202.3	279
	Minimal number of book-units (110 per pupil)		22,253	30,690
			231.3	310.8
2d-level teachers	Number of teachers	53.6		
	Minimal number of book units (700 per teacher)	37,520	161,910	217,560

SOURCE: UNESCO, "Assessment of Africa's Book Needs," COM/CS/68/3/5/ Add., pp. 19–20 (Meeting of Experts on Book Development in Africa, Accra, February 13–19, 1968).

[a] Book stock needs shown in this column *do not* represent book stocks actually existing in 1965, but are merely an indication, for purposes of comparison, of the level of stocks which would have been needed in 1965, according to minimal criteria.

[b] A breakdown by stages was not available for 1965. These figures thus correspond to the total number of pupils following regular training. Minimal criteria for book-units have, therefore, been calculated at 82 book-units.

As I have observed for Nigeria, so in other countries where there is publishing, a cadre of professional publishing personnel is being created. There is great opportunity here for European and American publishers to help, giving work-study scholarships to interested and promising young men and women. (This help should, of course, be extended to all the countries of the world—not just Africa alone—where publishing industries are crying for experienced workers.) It is important to bear in mind, however, that the training experience had best be in houses more nearly like those experienced in Africa. The

TABLE 4

DEVELOPMENT OF THIRD-LEVEL EDUCATION
AND BOOK NEEDS 1975–80 (IN THOUSANDS)

	1965 (base year)	1965	1980
Number of students	27.047	115	247
Minimal number of book-units (125 per student)	3,380	14,375	30,875
Number of teachers	3.809	13	15
Minimal number of book-units (900 per teacher)	3,428	11,700	13,500

SOURCE: UNESCO "Assessment of Africa's Book Needs,"
COM/CS/68/3/5/ Add., p. 21. (Meeting of Experts on Book
Development in Africa, Accra, February 13–19, 1968).
a Book stock needs in this column *do not* represent book stocks
actually existing in 1965, but are merely an indication, for purposes of comparison, of the level of stocks which would have
been needed in 1965 according to minimal criteria.

publishing environment in Africa is much more likely to be that of the small
press, where great versatility is required, rather than that of the large press
where rampant specialization would disable a trainee from effective work
under less sophisticated circumstances.

COOPERATIVE PUBLISHING AGREEMENTS

One of the great boons for publishing in Africa, and elsewhere in the
underdeveloped world, has been the Stockholm protocol to the Berne Copyright Convention. This protocol permits publishers in underdeveloped countries to use copyrighted materials which are important to them. There has been
much criticism of this protocol, but perhaps some broader perspective is required. Why should not the "have" publishers share freely with the "have not"
publishers? The creation of a literate world is in the interest of us all.

The United States is not signatory to the Berne Convention, nor with our
protectionist policies are we likely to be. But every publisher and every writer
who wishes to help in the illumination of the unpublishing Third World can do
so by writing into contracts clauses granting right of free access to their
materials published in these countries for the purposes of education.

Other forms of cooperation are also possible. For example, Northwestern
University Press has actively sought out ways of working with African presses,
and as a result is the American distributor for the books of the Mbari Artists
and Writers Club, for *Black Orpheus,* for the East African Publishing House,
and for the Haile Sellassie I University Press. With many of these houses, it is

fair to say, the act of co-publishing is critically important in the initial phases. The same is true of the University of Ife Press (Nigeria), with whom present plans call for joint publication with Northwestern University Press of several art and archaeological books under the sponsorship of the Department of Antiquities of the Federal Government of Nigeria.

Above all what is needed is good and generous action. There have no doubt been enough conferences on African publishing, attended by pretty much the same cadres of people year after year and producing nearly identical conclusions, yet little publishing development for Africa. What is required is fresh and creative thought and action. Making African literary materials available and expanding African markets by distributing books in Europe and America are just two initial, halting steps. There is little doubt that most conferences on African publishing have been too greatly dominated by the concept of *development*– an important concept to be sure, and a desirable and inevitable process. But it does tend to preclude the areas of creative cultural expression. *Development,* it must be borne in mind, is often an *externally* conceived and funded activity. While it may have the support of administrators in African countries who have goals identical with those of the economists, educationalists, planners, and other social scientists who espouse developmentism, it is important to assess the extent and manner in which these goals are relevant to the various African cultures. There is often something ethnocentric about *development,* and often something narrow in the perspective of a trans-national elite of social experts.

In terms of the growth of publishing in Africa this stress on development leads one to wonder whether the African publishing industry will respond to the projected need for books. One sometimes gets the impression that what the planners foresee is a burgeoning of Prentice-Halls and McGraw-Hills, and if the developers have their way this may be what will happen. Whether such houses will do more than *develop,* whether they will, as dynamic publishing houses should, contribute to the arts and the delights of the mind—to the articulation of national cultures—is, I think, a moot question. What is required in Africa is the growth of publishing houses organically conceived and evolved as an inevitable part of the culture. East African Publishing House, with its diverse publishing activities, should perhaps more nearly constitute the model for African publishing than the great American textbook house.

BOOK PUBLISHERS IN SUB-SAHARAN AFRICA

Cameroon

Au Frères Réunis. Douala
Basel Mission Book Depot. Victoria

Cameroon Protestant College. Mankon Bamenda

Diffusion Internationale Camerounaise de Livre et de la Presse. Sangmelima
Editions C.L.E. § ‡ Yaoundé
John Holt. Victoria
Librairie Fraternelle Luthérienne. Garoua
Librairie du Peuple Africain. Yaoundé
Librairie Saint-Paul. Youndé

Congo Republic (Brazzaville)

Procure de l'Archevêché. Brazzaville
Société Africaine de Libraire Papeterie (SALP). Brazzaville.
Société Congolaise Hachette. Brazzaville

Democratic Republic of the Congo (Kinshasa)

Agence Congolaise Hachette. Kinshasa
Librairie Evangelique au Congo (LECO). Kinshasa
Librairie Institut Politique Congolais. Kinshasa
Librairie Papeterie Rassaert. Lubumbashi

Dahomey

Librairie du Benin. Cotonou
Librairie Protestante. Cotonou

Ethiopia

Haile Sellassie I University Press.† Addis Ababa
International Press Agency. Addis Ababa
Menno Bookstore. Addis Ababa
Oxford University Press. § Addis Ababa

Ghana

Anowuo Educational Publishers. § Accra
Asamoah. Tamale
Bureau of Ghana Languages. Accra
Gasarm Partners. Accra
Ghana Daily Graphic (Book Shop). Accra
Ghana University Press. Accra
Longman Group Ltd. § Accra
Methodist Book Depot. Cape Coast
Presbyterian Book Depot. Accra
Reliance Trading Stores. Koforidua
State Publishing Corp. Accra
University Bookshop (University College of Cape Coast). Cape Coast
University Bookstore (University of Ghana). Legon
University Bookstore. Kumasi

Kenya

British Tutorial College (Africa) Ltd. Nairobi
City Bookshop. Mombasa
The E.A. Standard Ltd. Nairobi
East African Insitute Press. § Nairobi
East African Literature Bureau. § Nairobi
East African Newspapers. Nairobi
East African Publishing House.† Nairobi
Equatorial Publishers. § Nairobi
Heinemann Educational Books Ltd. § Nairobi
Longman Kenya Ltd. § Nairobi
Oxford University Press. § Nairobi
Patwa News Agency Ltd. Nairobi
Premier Bookshop. Nairobi
Samcas Book Services Ltd. Nairobi
Stationery & Office Supplies Ltd. Nairobi

Supermarkets Ltd. Nairobi

University Press of Africa (Quality Publications Ltd.). Nairobi

Liberia

Captain's Bookshop. Monrovia

University Bookstore (University of Liberia). Monrovia

Mozambique

A. W. Bayly & Co. Ltd. Lourenço Marques

Empresa Moderna Ltd. Lourenço Marques

M. Salema & Carvalho Lda. Beira

Spanos Commercial Lda. Beira

D. Spanos Sucrs. Lda. Lourenço Marques

Nigeria

Abimbola Bookshops. Lagos

Adiele Alia Modern Book Shops. Port Harcourt

African Development Bookshops. Ibadan

African Education Press (University of Lagos).* Yaba

African Universities Press.* Lagos

Aideyan Brothers Bookshops. Benin City

Akinrimisi Surulere Bookshops. Ondo

Akintoroye Ibudun Oluwa Bookshops. Ondo

Benevolent Bookshops. Ibadan

Book & Press Distribution. Lagos

Bookworm Co. Yaba

Brothers. Aba

C.M.S. (Nigeria) Bookshops. Lagos

Cambridge University Press. Ibadan

Chuks' Bookshops. Yaba

The Daily Times. Lagos

Daystar Press.* Ibadan

Department of Antiquities (Federal Government).§ Lagos

Design Productions W.A. Yaba

Diwes Bookshops. Port Harcourt

Enterprise Development Company.* Lagos

Etudo Press.* Onitsha

Evans Brothers Ltd. Ibadan

Falafin Publishers.* Yaba

Fakunle Major Services Press.* Oshogbo

Fellowship Bookshops Ltd. Port Harcourt

Fola Publishing Company. Abeokuta

Gamu Olubukun Bookshops. Lagos

Gaskiya Press.* Yaba

Grace Bookshops. Lagos

Guinea Coast Publications (Yaba Academy)* Yaba

Heinemann Educational Books Ltd.* Ibadan

Ibadan University Press.‡ Ibadan

International Press.* Aba

Invincible Bookshop. Lagos

John West Publications Ltd.* Lagos

Kingsway Stores KTD. Lagos

Ladesuyi Iwalewa Store & Bookshops. Ilesha

Longman Nigeria Ltd. Ikeja

Macmillan & Co. Ltd. Ibadan

Mbari (The Writers and Artists Club). §† Ibadan

Megida Printers & Publishers. Yaba

New Nigeria Press.* Ebute Metta

Nigerian Baptist Book Store. Ibadan

Nigerian National Press.* Apapa

Northern Nigerian Publishing Co.* Zaria

Olatunbosun Independent Bookshops. Ibadan

Onibonoje Educational Press.* Ibadan

Onwuamaegbu Bachon Bookshops. Port Harcourt
Oxford University Press. Ibadan
Pilgrim Books Ltd.* Lagos
Rational Bookshop. Ibadan
Scientific & Literary Publishing Co.* Ikeja
Speedwell Books Ltd. Yaba
Sudan Interior Mission Bookshops (S.I.M.). Jos
Tabansi Enterprises.* Onitsha
Thomas Nelson & Sons Ltd. Apapa
Town and Gown Publishers.* Yaba
United Nigeria Bookshop. Benin City
University Bookshop Nigeria Ltd. (University of Ibadan). Ibadan.
University Company Bookshop. Lagos
University of Ife Press. § † Ile-Ife
University of London Press.* Ibadan
University of Nigeria Press Ltd. Nsukka
Varsity Press.* Onitsha
Western Zone Bookshops. Benin City.
William Collins Sons & Co.* Akure

Senegal

Institut Fondemental d'Afrique Noire (IFAN). § Dakar

Sierra Leone

Longman Group Ltd. § Freetown

Sudan

Abdelmoneim Publishing Co. Khartoum
Al Bashir Bookshop. Khartoum
Amon Bookshop. Khartoum
Central Stationery & Bookshop. Khartoum

Dayaram & Sons. Port Sudan
The Khartoum Bookshop. Khartoum
Port Sudan Bookshop. Port Sudan
Publications Bureau. Khartoum
Sudan Bookshop. Khartoum

Tanzania

Cathedral Bookshop. Dar es Salaam
Dar Es Salaam Bookshop. Dar es Salaam
Longman Tanzania Ltd. § Dar es Salaam
Tanganyika Standard. Dar es Salaam
Tanzania Publishing House Ltd. Dar es Salaam
University College Bookshop. Dar es Salaam

Togo

Librairie bon Marché. Lomé
Librairie de l'Ecole Professionelle. Lomé
Librairie Evangelique. Lomé
Librairie Populaire du Togo. Lomé
Walter et Cie. Lomé

Uganda

East African Standard Ltd. Kampala
Patel Press Ltd. Kampala
Transition Books. § ‡ Kampala
Uganda Argus Ltd. Kampala
Uganda Bookshop. Kampala
Uganda Printing & Publishing Company Ltd. Kampala
Uganda Publishing House. § Kampala
University Bookshop (Makerere University College). Kampala

Upper Volta

Librairie Imprimerie Evangélique.

Ougadougou

Librairie Evangelique Assemble de Dieu. Ougadougou

Librairie Jeunesse d'Afrique. Ougadougou

Librairie de la Mission Catholique. Ougadougou

S.A.E.R.O. Import-Export. Ougadougou

Zambia

Bonse Pamo Bookshop. Fort Roseberry

Catholic Bookshop. Lusaka

Kingston's Ltd. Lusaka

Kingston's (North) Ltd. Ndola

Longman Zambia Ltd. § Lusaka

Oxford University Press. § Lusaka

SOURCE: The basic list was compiled in *Publishers World 69–70* (New York: R. R. Bowker, 1969), pages 165–66. Some of these publishers are, in all probability, only occasionally involved in book publishing.

* means that the entry was taken from Franklin Book Programs, Inc.,"A Book Development Project In Nigeria 1964–68" (a report submitted to the Ford Foundation), pages 197–99.

§ means that the entry has been supplied by the author.

† means that books are distributed in the United States of America by Northwestern University Press.

‡ means that books are distributed in the United States of America by Africana Publishing Corp.

3

African Newspapers and Periodicals

HANS E. PANOFSKY and ROBERT KOESTER

AFRICAN NEWSPAPERS AND JOURNALS not only give us the most up-to-date information about their respective topics or countries of publication but are also a primary source for further analysis by students as well as writers of textbooks and research publications.

African newspapers, with the exception of some in Egypt (such as *al-Ahram*) and South Africa (such as the *Rand Daily Mail),* tend to be small in size and usually reflect government policy. The so-called independent newspapers, which are frequently larger, are generally controlled by expatriates. Most African newspapers reprint extensively the press releases of their government and often releases by other governments as well. Some can afford to subscribe to international wire services. Their staffs tend to be small—too small to permit a great deal of individual reporting. Newspapers are generally printed at least partially in English, French, or Arabic, although there are daily papers in Swahili and Hausa and newspapers of less-than-daily frequency in other African languages.

African newspapers are usually published in the country's capital and frequently do not circulate much outside the capital area. Their small circulation figures, however, must not be used to estimate their impact. And although this impact is primarily among the literate sections of the community, newspapers are often read aloud to nonreaders.

American college and university libraries do not find it easy to subscribe to African newspapers, which are basically printed for immediate, local consumption; in addition, American libraries are frequently reluctant to subscribe to daily newspapers from abroad. There are, however, several libraries which do subscribe. These are listed in *African Newspapers in Selected American Libraries* (revised by the Library of Congress in 1965, available from the Superintendent of Documents, United States Government Printing Office, for 75 cents). This list includes the newspaper titles that have been microfilmed by the Library of Congress and the Association of Research Libraries' Foreign Newspaper Microfilm Project (administered by the Center for Research Libraries in Chicago);

it does not include the extensive South African titles purchased by the University of Massachusetts from Microfile in Johannesburg. A recent listing of newspapers and periodicals on Africa in microform has been compiled by Joan Ells and published in the *African Studies Bulletin,* XII(1969), 193–210.

Some journals pertaining to Africa go back to the mid-nineteenth century. They were until quite recently the sole vehicles of fact and opinion of more-or-less professional expatriate Africanists. With independence and growing literacy in Africa, the situation is changing.

One of the earliest journal titles is the *Anti-slavery Reporter and Aborigines' Friend,* which began in London in 1840. A few decades later, as a memorial to Mary Kingsley, there was started what is now known as *African Affairs,* a relatively popular journal for English people who want to go, or already have been, to Africa. In 1917 a journal was established representing British commercial and political interests, *West Africa,* a weekly which is still published in London with the aid of many African reporters in the field. There are less distinguished journals of this type for East and South Africa.

In 1929 the first scholarly journal was begun: *Africa,* published by the International African Institute in London. Two years later the comparable *Journal de la Société des Africanistes* was established in Paris. Missionary journals prior to these dates, however, did include scholarly articles on Africa. More recently, the Belgians have produced *Zaïre,* a scholarly journal in French which was published from 1947 to 1961 (one year after Congolese independence).

With the coming of African independence, there was a dramatic increase in African journalism and scholarly publishing. A link between earlier times and the current scene is *Présence Africaine,* which was first published in Paris in 1947 by the Senegalese editor who still edits it today.

At present, three literary journals deserve special mention: *Abbia,* published in Cameroon; *Black Orpheus,* published in Ibadan; and *Transition,* from Uganda, whose publication has been suspended.

The publication in the United States of journals about Africa is extremely limited, with one important exception: *African Arts/Arts d'Afrique.* This quarterly has been issued by the African Studies Center at the University of California, Los Angeles, since 1967. Other American publications of note are *Africa Report,* a nine-times-a-year magazine (which changed editorship in November, 1969, and now regards itself as a forum for opinion), and *Africa Today,* a more-or-less monthly which is somewhat left of center. There is, however, no major scholarly journal on Africa published in the United States. *The African Studies Bulletin* serves essentially as the house-organ of the (United States) African Studies Association. In Canada there is a *Canadian Journal of African Studies,* which was begun in 1967.

Probably the best journals specifically serving the Africanist community are *Africa* (London), the *Journal of African History* and the *Journal of Modern African Studies* (both published by Cambridge University Press, the former the major historical journal in English, the latter dealing mainly with economics and political science), and two other journals with a similar focus: *Cahiers d'Études Africaines* (Paris) and *Geneve-Afrique*. We must remember, however, that a growing number of scholarly articles on Africa are published in the scholarly journals of particular disciplines. Such disciplinary journals are increasingly appearing in Africa.[1] *Serials for African Studies,* issued by the Library of Congress in 1961 (a new edition is in preparation), lists over 2,000 journal titles.

In addition to serials dealing specifically with Africa, one must also consider those periodicals which are organized around particular issues or disciplines but which include, as a matter of course, a significant number of articles pertaining to Africa. The following titles are offered only as a highly selective list. The frequency with which writings about Africa appear in them is high, they are easily available and obtainable, and most of them are indexed in the standard periodical guides (e.g., *Reader's Guide, Social Sciences and Humanities Index,* and *Public Affairs Information Service*). These include *American Anthropologist, American Behavioral Scientist, American Historical Review, American Journal of Archaeology, American Journal of Sociology, American Political Science Review, American Sociological Review, Annals of the American Academy of Political and Social Science, Annals of the Association of American Geographers, Anthropological Quarterly, Anthropos, Antiquity, British Journal of Sociology, Civilisations, Current History, Economic Geography, Ethnomusicology, Foreign Affairs, Geographical Review, Government and Opposition, Homme, Industrial and Labor Relations Review, International Affairs, International Labor Review* (ILO), *Journal of American Folklore, Journal of Comparative Studies, Journal of Conflict Resolution, Journal of Economic and Social Development, Journal of Economic History, Journal of Politics, Journal of the Developing Area, Journal of World Politics, Language* (Journal of the Linguistic Society of America), *Man, Mid-East, Mizan, Mundus, PMLA* (Publications of the Modern Language Society of America), *School of Oriental and African Studies Bulletin, Social Research, Southwestern Journal of Anthropology, Western Political Quarterly, World Affairs, World Politics,* and *UNESCO Courier.*

We have appended four selected listings to this essay: (1) general journals pertaining to Africa; (2) African journals relevant to particular parts or modules of the *Syllabus;* (3) high-quality Africana journals arranged according to country; and (4) major African newspapers. In most cases we have followed a presentation format similar to the other reference formats in this volume:

1.Name of journal.

---

1. In geography alone, for example, these include the following: *Bulletin de la Societe de Geographie d' Alger et de l'Afrique du Nord* (published in Algiers), *Bulletin of the Ghana Geographical Association* (Accra), *Bulletin de la Societe de Geographie d'Egypte* (Cairo), *East African Geographical Review* (Kampala), *Ethiopian Geographical Journal* (Addis Ababa), *Revue de Geographie Marocaine* (Rabat), *Madagascar: Revue de Geographie* (Tananarive), *Nigerian Geographical Journal* (Ibadan), *South African Geographical Journal* (Johannesburg), and *The Bulletin: Journal of the Sierra Leone Geographical Association* (Freetown).

2. Publisher and address, date of original publication, and number of publications per year.

3. Brief annotation as to scholarly level and substantive focus.

I: SELECTED GENERAL JOURNALS ON AFRICA

Africa Quarterly
5 Balvantary Mehta Lane, New Delhi at Everest Press, Delhi 6.
1961—.
  Broadly covers the social sciences and humanities providing an Indian perspective on African studies.

Africa Report
866 United Nations Plaza, New York, New York 10017. 1956—, monthly.
  News analysis and coverage; regular features on the arts, critical book essay-reviews; new "Dialog" section provides opportunity for different opinions on a current topic.

African Abstracts
International African Institute, St. Dunstan's Chambers, 10/11 Fetter Lane, London EC4. 1950—, quarterly.
  An index/abstract of anthropological, sociological, and political studies.

African Affairs
Oxford University Press, Press Road, Neasden, London NW10.
1901—, quarterly.
  The major popular British journal of African studies.

Bulletin de l'IFAN
Institut Fondamental d'Afrique Noire, B.P. 206, CCP Dakar 5200, Senegal.
1939-1953; Series A: natural sciences, 1954—, quarterly; Series B: human sciences, 1954—, quarterly.
  One of the very best journals in African studies. The first series covers the natural sciences; the second, history, archaeology and anthropology, linguistics, geography, and bibliographies and documents.

Cahiers d'Études Africaines
Mouton & Co., P.O. Box 1132, The Hague, Netherlands. 1960—, quarterly.
  Important historical and social scientific work in French and English.

Genève-Afrique
Institut Africain de Geneve, 2-4, route de Drize, 1227 Carouge-Genève, Switzerland.
  Articles on the historical and social sciences; important bibliographies. In French and English.

Journal de la Société des Africanistes
Musée de l'Homme, Place du Trocadero, Paris 16e. 1931 –, irregular.
> One of the most prestigious continuing serials in the field; extensive bibliographies.

Journal of Modern African Studies
Cambridge University Press, Cambridge, England. 1963 –, quarterly.
> Political, economic, and social development in Africa today.

Nigerian Journal of Economic and Social Studies
Nigerian Economic Society, University of Ibadan, Ibadan, Nigeria. 1959 –, monthly.
> Articles and reviews, notes and communications on Nigerian and African economics and other social sciences.

Odu, a Journal of West African Studies (Ife, Nigeria)
Oxford University Press Warehouse, 10-12 Warehouse Road, P.O. Box 160, Apapa, Nigeria. 1964 –, biennial.
> Excellent new journal of arts, history, and cultural affairs.

Présence Africaine
25 bis, rue des Écoles, Paris 5e. 1947 –, quarterly.
> A bilingual review on African history, literature, and arts; one of the most important and influential journals on the continent.

Translations on Africa
Clearinghouse for Federal Scientific and Technical Information, Springfield, Va. 22151. 1964 –, semimonthly.
> Translations into English of important articles in all fields (primarily social sciences) from Africanist journals in French, Portuguese, etc.

West African Review
Overseas Newspapers (Agencies) Ltd., Cromwell House, Fulwood Place, London W.C.1. Liverpool, 1922- 1962, monthly.
> Agriculture, religion, economics, law, general.

Zaïre: revue Congolaise
Éditions Universitaires, Brussels. 1947-61.
> An important general scholarly magazine; bilingual.

II: SELECTED JOURNALS ARRANGED BY SYLLABUS MODULES

Part I: African Society and Culture

General

Africa

International African Institute, St. Dunstan's Chambers, 10/11 Fetter Lane, London, EC4. 1928 — , quarterly.

Anthropology, ethnology, folklore, linguistics, demography, current research, bibliography.

11. Language and Linguistic Systems

African Language Studies
London, School of Oriental and African Studies, University of London. 1960 — .

Scholarly articles on sub-Saharan languages.

Afrika und Übersee
Dietrich Reimer, Verlag, Berlin 45, Drakestrasse 40 (West Berlin). 1910 — , irregular.

Largely devoted to African linguistics and culture; articles in English, French, and German.

Journal of African Languages
Department of Linguistics, Michigan State University, East Lansing, Mich. 1962 — .

Scholarly articles on African language, linguistics, and literature. Book reviews.

Journal of West African Languages
Cambridge University Press, Cambridge, England. 1964 — , semiannual.

Articles in English and French on West African languages and linguistics.

Swahili, Journal of the Institute of Swahili Research
Institute of Swahili Research, P.O. Box 35091, Dar es Salaam, Tanzania. Semiannual.

Contributions on Swahili language, literature, linguistics, and language teaching. Articles in English, Swahili, French, and German.

13. Conceptual Systems and Religion

Cahiers des religions africaines
B.P. 867 Kinshasa XI. 1967 — , semiannual.

Results of "research conducted to obtain a scientific understanding of African religions, beliefs and customs, both traditional and modern, and to provide food for thought to African theologians and men of culture."

Orita, Ibadan Journal of Religious Studies
Department of Religious Studies, University of Ibadan, Ibadan, Nigeria. 196? — , irregular.

Aims to contribute to an "interpretation and understanding of African traditional religion, Christianity, and Islam," both in themselves and in their relationships.

14. Visual Arts

African Arts/Arts d'Afrique
University of California, Los Angeles, California 90024. 1967 – , quarterly.
Graphic, plastic, performing, and literary arts; handsome and scholarly; many color illustrations.

Part II: Perspectives on the Past

General

African Historical Studies
The African Studies Center, Boston University, 10 Lenox Street, Brookline, Mass. 02146. 1968 – , semiannual.
Scholarly articles, book reviews, news, and notes.

Journal of African History
Cambridge University Press, Cambridge, England. London, 1960 – , quarterly.
History, cultural anthropology, critical book reviews.

Journal of the Historical Society of Nigeria
Historical Society of Nigeria, jointly with the Ibadan University Press, Ibadan, Nigeria. 1956 – .
Articles, research notes, and reviews; especially important for research on Nigerian history but also covering other West Africa areas.

Tarikh
Ibadan, Longman. 1965 – , semiannual.
Historical articles by scholars "for students, teachers, and the general reader." Excellent for college level.

Transactions of the Historical Society of Ghana
Department of History, University of Ghana, Legon, Accra, Ghana. 1952 – , irregular.
Historical essays on Ghana, West Africa, and the continent as a whole.

The West African Archeological Newsletter (to become the *West African Journal of Archeology* in 1970)
Institute of African Studies, University of Ibadan, Ibadan, Nigeria. 1964– 1969.
This new journal promises to publish excavation reports and other primary data as well as articles of archaeological synthesis of larger conception. West African material will have priority, but other areas and issues will be considered.

20. Early Culture and State Formation

Journal of Egyptian Archeology
The Egypt Exploration Society, 2-3 Dought Mews, London, WC1. 1914—,
irregular.

> Primarily concerned with Egyptology, papyrology, and archaeology, but
> also with historical records from the Sudan.

Part III: Processes of Change

41. Personality and Social Change

Psychopathologie Africaine
Société Générale de Banques au Senegal; compte ban caire: 30920, Dakar
(subscriptions); Société de Psychopathologie et d'Hygiene Mentale de Dakar
(publisher). 1965—, irregular.

> Articles in English and French on African psychiatry, psychopathology,
> psychology, and sociology.

42. Educational Systems in Africa

Teacher Education in New Countries
Oxford University Press, Press Road, Neasden, London NW10. 1960—, 3 times
a year.

> Disseminates information about activities of institutes and faculties of educa-
> tion and the problems of teaching in developing countries; covers Asia, the
> Caribbean, and elsewhere, as well as Africa.

West African Journal of Education
Institute of Education, University of Ibadan, Ibadan, Nigeria. 1957—, 3 times
a year.

> Articles devoted to teaching, curricula, texts.

46. The Nature of Urban Life

African Urban Notes
African Studies Center, Michigan State University, East Lansing, Mich. 48823.
1966—, occasional.

> Research news and articles on urban studies in Africa.

48. Spatial Aspects of Transportation and Communications

Nigerian Geographical Journal
Nigerian Geographical Association. 1957—, irregular.

One of the best journals of African geography. See the footnote on page 33 for other geographical journals.

49. New Modes of Communication

Bingo
11 rue de Teheran, Paris 8e. Dakar, 1953 — , monthly.
"A monthly review of black activity." Written for popular consumption in Africa.

Drum
Drum Publications (Nigeria) Ltd., P.M.B. 2128, Lagos, Nigeria. 1951 — , monthly. Various editions, e.g. P.O. Box 1197, Accra, Ghana; P.M.B. 2128, Lagos, Nigeria.
Africa's most popular magazine.

Spear
East African Railways and Harbours, P.O. Box 30121, Nairobi, Kenya. 1952 — , bimonthly.
A pictorial popular magazine of general interest.

50. The Impact of Christianity

Journal of Religion in Africa
E.J. Brill, Leiden, Netherlands. 1968 — , 3 times a year.
"Devoted to the scientific study of the forms and history of religion, within the African continent (and in sub-Saharan Africa in particular)." Important bibliographical contributions.

Orita, Ibadan Journal of Religious Studies (see under Module 13, above)

51. Innovation, Synthesis, and Independency

Journal of Religion in Africa (see under Module 50, above)

Orita, Ibadan Journal of Religious Studies (see under Module 13, above)

52. Islamic Reformation Movements

Journal of Religion in Africa (see under Module 50, above)

Orita, Ibadan Journal of Religious Studies (see under Module

Research Bulletin, Centre of Arabic Documentation
University of Ibadan, Centre of Arabic Doc., Institute of African Studies, Ibadan, Nigeria. 1964 — , biennial.

Articles, research notes and reviews on the work at the Center; primarily concerned with African Islamic history and thought.

Part IV: Consolidation of Nation-States

General

Africa Research Bulletin
Africa House, Kingsway, London WC2. 1964 – , monthly.
  Intensive and extensive selections and summaries, news of Africa from the press and government documents; issued in two series: political, social, and cultural; and economic, financial, and technical.

Africa Digest
2 Arundel Street, London WC2. 1952 – , bimonthly.
  News and book reviews taken from the world press; arranged by country.

Africa Confidential
5/33 Rutland Gate SW7, London.
  A newsletter on current political events with "inside" information which is not for distribution.

l'Afrique et l'Asie
Imprimerie Administrative Centrale, 8 rue de Furstenberg, Paris 6e. 1948 – , quarterly.
  Contributions concerned with politics, economics, and other social sciences.

American Universities Field Staff Report Service, African Series
American Universities Field Staff, Inc., 366 Madison Avenue, New York, N.Y. 10017.
  A series of monographic case-study pamphlets, issued irregularly, on the regions and countries of Africa, written by experts for the generalist. Attempts an overview of specific nation-building problems.

Chronologie politique africaine
Fondation Nationale des Sciences Politiques, 27 rue Saint-Guillaume, Paris 7e. 1960 – , bimonthly.
  A day-by-day record of political events; arranged by geographical region with a subject index.

East Africa Journal
Uniafric House, Koinange Street, P.O. Box 30571, Nairobi, Kenya. 1964 – , monthly.
  A magazine of opinion on politics, education, and contemporary affairs.

Journal of African and Asian Studies

E. J. Brill, Leiden, Netherlands. 1967 — .
Contributions, both theoretical and case-descriptive, mainly by Indian authors on sociopolitical and economic development in the Third World.

Journal of Asian and African Studies
Department of Sociology, York University, Toronto, Ontario. 1966 — , quarterly.
Studies of man and society in the developing nations; endeavors to unite research in the social sciences to build up systematic knowledge for use in the reconstruction of societies entering a phase of advanced technology.

Revue française d'études politiques africaines, "Le Mois en Afrique"
Société Africaine d'Edition, 32 rue de l'Echiquier, Paris 10e. 1966 — , monthly.
Analysis of recent important political events; studies on a particular theme each month; bibliographies.

West Africa
Overseas Newspapers (Agencies) Ltd., Cromwell House, Fulwood Place, London WC1. 1917 — , weekly.
Current events, economy, political analyses, book reviews.

60. The Role of Ideology in Nation-Building

Africa and the World
89 Fleet Street, London, EC4. 1965 — , monthly.
News and opinion issued by Kwame Nkrumah and his supporters-in-exile in London.

62. Institutions and Bureaucracy

Administration
Institute of Administration, P.M.B. 5246, Ibadan, Nigeria. Ife, Nigeria, 1966 — , quarterly.
Articles, news, book reviews on public administration and management, largely Nigerian case studies.

Cahiers africains d'administration publique/African Administrative Studies
Centre Africain de Formation et de Recherche Administratives pour le Developpement (CAFRAD) B.P. 310, Tangier, Morocco.
.Studies, documents, news, and bibliographical notes from the Centre.

Sudan Journal of Administration and Development
P.O. Box 1492, Khartoum. 1965 — , annual.
Public administration training and research in Africa are its focal points. In English and Arabic.

67. *The Integration of Legal Systems*

African Law Studies
African Law Center, Box 58, 435 W. 116th Street, New York, N.Y. 10027.
1969–, quarterly.
   "Bibliographical essays, analysis of comparable legislation; . . . surveys of legal developments in particular countries or . . . fields."

East African Law Journal
Legal Publications, P.O. Box 7148, Nairobi, Kenya. 1965–, quarterly.
   Articles, commentary, case notes, legislative news, and book reviews dealing with law in Kenya, Tanzania, and Uganda.

Journal of African Law
Butterworth & Co. Ltd., 88 Kingsway, London WC2. 1957–, 3 times a year.
   Legal studies on the African countries.

Nigerian Law Journal
African Universities Press, P.O. Box 1287, Lagos, Nigeria. 1964–, annual.
   Articles and surveys of legal developments in Nigeria.

68. *The Development of Constitutional Law*

African Law Digest
African Law Center, Box 58, 435 W. 116th Street, New York, N.Y. 10027.
1965–, quarterly.
   "A compilation, in digest form, of the significant legislation, administrative regulations and notices of the states and territories of Africa together with notes and other items of interest."

70. *Agricultural Reorganization*

Bulletin of Rural Economics and Sociology
Ibadan University Press, Ibadan, Nigeria. 1964–, irregular.
   Research studies in agricultural extension, rural economics, and sociology carried out by staff members of the Department of Agricultural Economics and Extension, University of Ibadan.

71. *The Industrialization Process*

Manpower and Unemployment Research in Africa
Centre for Developing Area Studies, McGill University, Montreal, Quebec.
1968–.
   A newsletter presenting short research notes on this specialized topic.

73. *Development of Economic Systems*

African Development

John Carpenter House, John Carpenter Street, London, EC4. 1967 — , monthly.

News, statistics, forecasts on African business, finance, and development.

Banque centrale des États de l'Afrique de l'Ouest: Notes d'information et statistiques
29 Rue du Colisée, Paris 8e. 1956(?) — , monthly.

Summaries of statistical information, financial and business news, and legislative developments affecting investment in Africa.

East African Economic Review
Oxford University Press, P.O. Box 12532, Nairobi, Kenya. 1954 — , semiannual.
"Economic problems of developing economies" are discussed in scholarly articles and book reviews.

Economic Bulletin for Africa (ECA)
United Nations, New York, N.Y. 1961 — .
Reports and surveys of financial, industrial, and economic development in Africa.

Journal of Business and Social Studies
University of Lagos, Lagos, Nigeria. 1968 — , semiannual.
"Scholarly works of social, political and economic interest particularly to Nigeria and other developing nations."

New Africa (Africa Trade and Development)
58 Paddington Street, London W1. 196? — , bimonthly.
News and opinion on politics and its relation with business and trade.

75. Technology and Nation-Building

Bulletin of the Regional Center for Science and Technology for Africa (UNESCO)
P.O. Box 30592, Nairobi, Kenya. 1966 — , quarterly.
Short articles devoted to recent developments in agriculture, natural resource use, health, technical education, etc. in Africa.

Journal of the West African Science Association
P.O. Box 4089, Ibadan, Nigeria. 1954 — , semiannual.
Studies in the biological and agricultural sciences.

Part V: Africa and the Modern World

General

African Forum
American Society for African Culture, New York, N.Y. 1965–67, quarterly.
Contemporary affairs for Africans and Afro-Americans; cultural, political.

Jeune Afrique

Presse Africaine Associée, 51 avenue des Ternes, Paris 17e. 1961(?)—, weekly.
A valuable, lively news magazine of fact and opinion; world events seen
from an African viewpoint.

Race
Institute of Race Relations, Oxford University Press, Press Road, Neasden
Lane, Neasden, London NW10. 1959—, semiannual.
Concentrates on contemporary race relations problems, especially those con-
cerning black men in America, Britain, Europe, and Africa.

79. Pan-Africanism and Continental Unity

OAU Review
Press and Information Department of OAU, P.O. Box 3243, Addis Ababa,
Ethiopia. 1968—, quarterly.
Journal tries to "reflect the life and aspiration of the Organization, its
struggle on all fronts for the total liberation of the African continent and the
economic, social and cultural advancement of its peoples."

Pan-African Journal
306 W. 93rd Street, Suite 35, New York, N.Y. 10025, 1968—, quarterly.
Aimed at promoting the expressions and thoughts of the African scholars in
poetry, literature, art, music, political, social, and economic matters of Africa
as well as issues of African unity.

80. International Organizations in Africa

Nations Nouvelles, Revue de l'OCAM
L'Organisation Commune Africaine et Malgache (OCAM), B.P. 437, Yaoundé,
Cameroon. 1962—, quarterly.
The official mouthpiece of the association of francophonic African states.

83. Africa and the United States

Africa Today
Graduate School of International Studies, University Park Campus, Denver,
Colo. 80210. 1953—, bimonthly.
Articles, commentary, book reviews; action oriented; concerned with South-
ern Africa and U.S. policy in the continent.

87. The Remnants of Colonialism

Mozambique Revolution
FRELIMO, Information Dept., 201 Nkrumah Street, P.O. Box 15274, Dar es
Salaam, Tanzania. Occasional publication.

The main organ of the Mozambique Liberation Front, formerly headed by
the late Dr. Eduardo Mondlane. News of the guerrilla war, interviews, press
reports, documents from this area.

Namibia News
South West African People's Organization (SWAPO), 10 Dryden Chambers,
119 Oxford Street, London W1. 1968 – , irregular.
A partisan newsletter designed to raise support for the liberation of
South-West Africa.

Zimbabwe Review
283 Grays Inn Road, London WC1. 1969 – , bimonthly.
Devoted to news and editorial opinion on the Zimbabwe (Southern Rhode-
sian) liberation movement.

88. Race Relations in Southern Africa

Thought
South African Institute of Race Relations, P.O. Box 97, Johannesburg. Irregu-
lar.
"A journal of Afrikaans thinking for the English-speaking."

Race Relations News
Auden House, 68 DeKorte Street, Johannesburg. 1938 – , quarterly.
Race relations problems in South Africa.

89. Politics and Race in South Africa

Black Sash
37 Harvard Buildings, Joubert Street, Johannesburg. 1956 – , monthly.
Organ of the Women's Defense of the Constitution League; one of the few
remaining white journals critical of the South African government.

Africa South in Exile (formerly *Africa South*)
1956– 1961.
Edited by Ronald Segal, this journal represented liberal/radical, primarily
white South African thought. Most contributors were exiles based in London.

90. Contemporary African Literature

African Literature Today
Heinemann Educational Books, 48 Charles Street, London. 1968 – , semiannual.
Articles, reviews, and bibliographies on the rich literary output of com-
temporary Africa.

Black Orpheus
Longman Nigeria, Ltd. P.M.B. 1036, Ikeja; Northwestern University Press, 1735 Benson Avenue, Evanston, Illinois 60201. 1957 —.
> The most important literary-artistic review published in Africa; stories, poetry, illustrations, reviews.

Busara
East African Publishing House, Ltd., P.O. Box 30571, Uniafric House, Koinange Street, Nairobi, Kenya. 1968 —, 3 times a year.
> Criticism, poetry, and fiction, largely from East Africa.

Cultural Events in Africa
The Transcription Centre, 6 Paddington Street, London W1. 1964 —, monthly.
> An important newsletter on literary, artistic, dramatic, and musical events and publications; interviews with authors, artists. and performers.

Journal of the New African Literature and the Arts
Oxford University Press, P.O. Box 12532, Government Road, Nairobi, Kenya. 1966 —, semiannual.
> Discussion and criticism of African creative works of art.

Mawazo
Makerere University College, F.O. Box 7062, Kampala, Uganda. 1967 —, quarterly.
> A general "intellectual" magazine concerned with politics, education and literature. Book reviews.

Okyeame
The Ghana Society of Writers, P.O. Box M. 15, Accra, Ghana. 1961 —, irregular.
> Ghana's principal literary magazine.

Transition
Kampala, Uganda. 1961– 1967.
> Primarily literary and political; editor recently released from prison; promises to resume publication.

91. Contemporary Social Thought

Ibadan
University of Ibadan, Ibadan, Nigeria. 1957 —, 3 times a year.
> A general, serious magazine, both discursive and creative, a sort of Nigerian *Partisan Review*.

Insight and Opinion
Insight Publications West Africa, P.O. Box 13, Cape Coast, Ghana. 1967(?) —, quarterly.

"An independent quarterly for socio-cultural, economic and political thought in the African context."

Mawazo (see under Module 90)

Transition (see under Module 90)

93. Visual Arts and Music

African Arts/Arts d'Africque (see under Module 14)

Cultural Events in Africa (see under Module 90)

Journal of the New African Literature and the Arts (see under Module 90)

94. Africa and Afro-American Identity

Crisis (NAACP)
Crisis Publishing Co., 20 W. 40th Street, New York, N. Y. 10018. 1910—,
   The official organ of the NAACP; occasional articles on Africa.

Journal of Negro History
Association for the Study of Negro Life and History, Inc., 1538 Ninth Street N.W., Washington, D.C. 20001. 1916—.
   Scholarly articles on Afro-American and African history, book reviews.

Liberator
Afro-American Research Institute, Inc., 244 E. 46th Street, New York, N. Y. 10017. 1961—, monthly.
   Analysis, opinion, and criticism of events and creations in the black world, both American and African.

Muhammad Speaks
436 E. 79th Street, Chicago, Ill. 60619. 1962—, biweekly.
   Official organ of the Nation of Islam, led by Elijah Muhammad. Often includes articles on Africa.

Negro Digest
1820 South Michigan Avenue, Chicago, Illinois, 60616. 1942—, monthly.
   A popular *Reader's Digest* type of magazine, featuring news articles, essays, and literature, many of them concerned with African Affairs.

Phylon
Atlanta University, 233 Chestnut Street, Atlanta, Ga. 30314. 1940—.
   Scholarly articles of anthropological, cultural, and historical interest, book reviews. Many articles on Africa.

95. Africa and Afro-American Social Change

The Black Panther

Ministry of Information, Box 2967, Custom House, San Francisco, California. Weekly.
   Partisan magazine of the Black Panther party.

99. Conducting Social Research in Africa

African Studies Bulletin
African Studies Center, Michigan State University, East Lansing, Mich. 1958 –, 3 times a year.
   Bibliographical essays; news of the (American) African Studies Association; research developments; library and archival descriptions; grant data.

Canadian Journal of African Studies
Loyola College, Montreal. 1967 –, 3 times a year.
   Largely Canadian contributions to the broad spectrum of African studies; special issues devoted to whole conference proceedings such as rural Africa.

100. Research Frontiers in Africa

African Notes
Institute of African Studies, Ibadan, Nigeria. 1963 –, quarterly.
   Excellent reports and articles on research-in-progress, particularly in archaeology, history, anthropology, etc.

African Social Research, formerly the *Rhodes-Livingstone Journal, Human Problems in Central Africa*
Institute for Social Research, University of Zambia, P.O. Box 900, Lusaka, Zambia. 1944 –, semiannual.
   Applied research in the social sciences, including history.

III: SELECTED JOURNALS ARRANGED BY COUNTRY

Botswana

Botswana Notes and Records
The Botswana Society, Private Bag 31, Gaberones, Botswana, S.A. 1969 –, quarterly.
   Articles concerned with history, archeology, culture and art in the former High Commission territories.

Cameroon

Abbia
Éditions C.L.E., B.P. 4048, Yaoundé, Cameroon. 1963 –, quarterly.
   Literary historical and artistic contributions in English and French.

Congo-Kinshasa

Études congolaises
Centre de Recherche et d'Information Socio-Politiques (C.R.I.S.P.), 35, rue du Congres, Bruxelles 1, Belgium. 1961—, quarterly.
    Studies on social scientific problems, reports of research, book reviews.

Kenya

Kenya Weekly News
D. A. Hawkins, Ltd., P.O. Box 2768, Nairobi, Kenya. 1928–1969.
    Covers all aspects of news in Kenya and East Africa in general. Read widely by Kenyan university students.

Reporter
News Publications Ltd., P.O. Box 30339, Nairobi, Kenya. Biweekly.
    Patterned after American news weeklies.

Liberia

Liberian Studies Journal
African Studies Center, DePauw University, Greencastle, Indiana 46135. 1968—, semiannual.
    History and social science research articles concerned with Liberia.

Morocco

Hespéris-Tamuda
l'Association des Sciences de l'Homme, 70 av. Abderrahman Aneggai, B.P. 447, Rabat, Morocco. Paris, 1921—, quarterly.
    Anthropology, history, and arts of the Maghrib.

Nigeria

Nigeria Magazine
Exhibition Centre, Marina, Lagos, Nigeria. 1934—, quarterly.
    A sophisticated yet popular magazine of culture, arts, literature, and general interest for those specifically interested in Nigeria. Excellent photographs.

Sierra Leone

Sierra Leone Studies
Fourah Bay College Bookshop, Mount Aureol, Freetown, Sierra Leone. 1953—, semiannual.
    General scholarly review.

Sudan

Sudan Notes and Records
Box 555, Khartoum, Sudan. 1918—, semiannual.

Important scholarly articles in all fields on the Sudan and other parts of Africa.

Tanzania

Tanzania Notes and Records
Tanzania Society, P.O. Box 511, Dar es Salaam, Tanzania. 1936 — , quarterly.
  Scholarly articles covering the sciences, social sciences, and humanities as they pertain to Tanzanian studies.

Uganda

Uganda Journal
The Uganda Society, Kampala, Uganda. 1934 — , semiannual.
  Articles on the life sciences, history, and ethnology of Uganda and East Africa.

IV: SELECTED NEWSPAPERS FROM AFRICA

Abidjan matin Abidjan, Ivory Coast, 1954(?) —

Afrique nouvelle, Dakar, Senegal, 1949 —

Cape Times, Cape Town, South Africa, 1876 —

Le Courrier d'Afrique, Kinshasa, Congo, 1930 —

Daily Graphic, Accra, Ghana, 1950 —

Daily Mail, Freetown, Sierra Leone, 1931 —

Daily Nation, Nairobi, Kenya, 1960 —

Daily Times, Lagos, Nigeria, 1925 —

East African Standard, Nairobi, Kenya, 1902 —

Egyptian Gazette, Cairo, U.A.R., 1880(?) —

L'Essor, Bamako, Mali, 1963(?) —

L'Essor du Katanga, Lubumbashi, Congo, 1928 —

Ethiopian Herald, Addis Ababa, Ethiopia, 1943 — , weekly

Fraternité matin, Abidjan, Ivory Coast, 1959 —

Gambia Echo, Bathurst, Gambia, 1934 —, weekly

Ghana Evening News, Accra, Ghana, 1948 —

Ghanaian Times, Accra, Ghana, 1958 —

Liberian Age, Monrovia, Liberia, 1946 —

The Nationalist, Dar es Salaam, Tanzania, 1964 —

New Nigerian, Kaduna, Nigeria, 1966 —

Rand Daily Mail, Johannesburg, South Africa, 1902 —

Rhodesia Herald, Salisbury, Rhodesia, 1891 —

Tanganyika Standard, Dar es Salaam, Tanzania, 1929 —

Le Temps du Niger, Niamey, Niger, 1960(?) —, weekly

The Times of Swaziland, Mbabane, Swaziland, 1896 —, weekly

Uganda Argus, Kampala, Uganda, 1912 —

West African Pilot, Lagos, Nigeria, 1937 —

Windhoek Advertiser, Windhoek, South-West Africa, 1919 —, semiweekly

4

African-Language Publications

AHMAD GETSO, MORRIS GOODMAN, JOSEPH MABWA, and JOHN PADEN

BEFORE WORLD WAR II, American undergraduate students were mainly limited in the study of modern languages to French, German, and Spanish (and, to a much lesser extent, Italian and Portuguese). This focus perhaps reflected a primary concern with Europe, and a peripheral interest in Latin America. After the war, there was a considerable increase in the number of foreign-language offerings at the university level. Russian and Eastern European languages made the greatest gains in the first postwar decade. Chinese, Japanese, Arabic, and other Far and Middle Eastern languages soon followed as these areas began to interest ever larger numbers of students and scholars. Even more recently, particularly after the independence of most of Africa in about 1960, certain of the major African languages (e.g., Swahili, Hausa, Amharic, and Yoruba) have come to be included in the curricula of many American universities.

This changing pattern of language selection at the American university level seems to indicate an extension of interest and concern from Europe to the world as a whole. It may also indicate a shift in the function of university-level language learning, away from the mere need to gain access to technical and scholarly writings in a foreign language (which are now often available in translation and in some cases are even translated by computer) toward the idea of communication with a particular culture zone in the world, whatever the level of its technical publications. Such communication can often be done effectively only in the language of that culture zone. In this essay we will try to suggest that a significant portion of the relevant literature regarding *The African Experience* has been published in African languages. We will try to illustrate this point by citing references in the two major sub-Saharan African languages, Hausa and Swahili. We have arranged these references according to the five substantive parts of the *Syllabus*. These references, with a few exceptions, are not available in English or French. Yet, while we fully support university-level African-language studies, we do not expect most American universities at this time to have the resources to offer such languages. Consequently, our selected references, all annotated in English, are intended primarily to illustrate some of the perimeters of Africana references which go beyond the French and English references. We will turn first, however, to a brief consideration of the distribution of African languages and literatures and then provide an overview of the study of such languages in Western institutions.

AFRICAN LANGUAGES AND LITERATURES

Although no definitive count exists, the languages of Africa almost certainly number over a thousand. Since the total African population (including the north) is probably close to 350 million, the average number of speakers per language is approximately 350,000. This figure, however, does not adequately convey the enormous range between the most and the least widely spoken. On the one hand, Arabic is spoken, with considerable dialectal variation, by over 50 million, concentrated almost exclusively in the north, and Hausa and Swahili, the two most widely spoken sub-Saharan languages, by 15 to 25 million each. On the other hand, many languages are spoken by 10,000 persons or less. There is some question, in fact, as to which of these speech communities represent languages and which merely dialects. Most linguists would say that two varieties of speech are dialects of the same language if they are mutually comprehensible, but are separate languages if they are not. This criterion is, admittedly, susceptible to different interpretations, since intelligibility between different speech forms is often partial and, in some cases, not reciprocal. Nevertheless, no matter how this criterion is applied, the minimal figure of 1,000 languages probably remains valid.

There are nonlinguists who may wish to restrict the designation "language" to those idioms which are written and standardized. By this standard, over 200 African languages are written to the extent that at least a part of the Bible has been translated into them and published. A much smaller number (probably less than 30 – e.g., Twi in Ghana, Yoruba in Nigeria, Zulu in South Africa, Luganda in Uganda, Malagasy in Madagascar) are regularly printed in the form of newspapers (dailies, weeklies, and monthlies), educational and religious material, etc. Most of these and probably some others have been used at one time or another as a language of instruction in schools at the lowest grades. A handful of these, such as Yoruba and Zulu, have been used as the vehicle of a modern creative literature. A great many languages which are not frequently written are regularly used in broadcasting.

Apart from Arabic, however, only three African languages may be considered at present to be functioning, standardized, literary languages: Swahili (the national language of Tanzania, generally understood throughout East Africa), Hausa (an official language in northern Nigeria, widely used in West Africa), and Amharic (the national language of Ethiopia). These are also among the largest language groups in Africa, with over 10 million speakers each. Of these Amharic has the oldest literary tradition, going back to the fourteenth century. It is written in the distinctive Ethiopian script which goes back even earlier (possibly fourth century A.D.) to ancient Ge'ez, the oldest literary language of Ethiopia, which is no longer spoken but continues to function as the liturgical and scholarly language of the Ethiopian church. This script is also used on occasion for some of the other languages of Ethiopia. Virtually all other written African languages now use the Latin alphabet. Earlier (at least since the eighteenth century) Hausa, Swahili, and a number of other African languages which came under strong Muslim influence were written in the Arabic script, and Arabic script (*ajami*) continues to be used for Hausa in addition to the Latin alphabet, even in printing. Indigenous scripts have been developed in sub-Saharan Africa. In the nineteenth century, the Vai of Liberia and the Bamum of Cameroon developed their own writing systems. Neither of these scripts, however, is widely used today.

THE STUDY OF AFRICAN LANGUAGES

Not only do some African languages have a written tradition of two hundred years or more, but the formal study of African languages likewise goes back a number of centuries. The earliest formal grammar of an African language, Kikongo (from which the Congo derives its name), was written in 1659 by an Italian priest, Brusciotto, who served as a missionary with the Portuguese. Toward the end of the seventeenth century a German scholar, Ludolf, produced grammars of two Ethiopian languages, ancient Ge'ez and Amharic. It was not until the nineteenth century, however, that intensive study of African languages by Europeans began, carried out by missionaries, explorers, administrators, and scholars. Among the most outstanding of these pioneers were Koelle in Sierra Leone, Bleek in South Africa, Krapf in East Africa, and Bishop Crowther, a Yoruba of Nigeria, who was the first to write a grammar of his native language.

It was not until the early twentieth century that formal instruction in African languages became regularly available in such institutions as the School of Oriental Studies (later, School of Oriental and African Studies—SOAS) in London and the Kolonialinstitut in Hamburg. Later, African languages came to be taught in a number of European and American institutions. Since the 1950s, the study of African languages has increased greatly in recognition of their growing importance. In the United States a number of universities have come to offer courses in a selection of African languages: UCLA, Northwestern, Wisconsin, Howard, Michigan State, Indiana, and Duquesne, for example. The number of American graduate students in African languages has been growing, particularly since the beginning of the 1960s when the federal government began to offer National Defense fellowships in a variety of African languages, and with the return of Peace Corps volunteers, many of whom were required to attain a certain level of proficiency in the language of their area prior to their two-year field assignments.

More recently, the espousal by many Black Studies programs of Swahili language study has led to a general revival of interest in that language. At Northwestern University during the 1969/70 academic year there were more than 60 undergraduate students (both white and black) enrolled in introductory Swahili classes. Whatever the role Swahili may come to play in Black Studies, it will also remain an important vehicle of the African experience in the eastern and central portions of the continent. Likewise, Hausa will probably remain the major lingua franca in West Africa. We summarize below some of the aspects of Hausa and Swahili literature which are most relevant to the thematic concerns of this volume, and we follow this with a list of selected Hausa and Swahili works.

HAUSA LITERATURE

According to A. H. M. Kirk-Greene, there are about 20 million persons in Nigeria and about 5 million persons outside of Nigeria who speak Hausa as a first or second language. Although the core area of Hausaland is in northern Nigeria (and southern portions of Niger Republic), Hausa is used as a lingua franca in many parts of West Africa. The language is related to Berber, although there are many Arabic loan words, particularly on matters related to Islamic culture. The major Hausa dictionary, by Bargery, contains about 60,000 words—although this may represent only about half of the entire language. Because Hausa was used as the official local language in Northern Nigeria during the colonial period, it has been relatively standardized in terms of spelling and grammar. There is a literary tradition in Hausa which extends back several centuries. Arabic script—called *ajami*—was used to write the language. In the twentieth century, the Latin alphabet—called *boko*—has been used extensively, and there has been a considerable increase in the number of writings available.

The illustrative list of Hausa published materials appended to this essay has been arranged into the five major categories of the *Syllabus* and the *Bibliography:* (1) Culture and Society (including Hausa stories and religious writings); (2) History; (3) Social Change; (4) Nation-Building (including political writings); and (5) Contemporary Literature. We present a brief overview of Hausa literature below, according to these categories. While there do exist some bilingual works in Hausa and English and some English translations of Hausa literature, it should be stressed that the vast bulk of Hausa literature has not been translated. In the selected list in this essay, only two items are also available in English.

Hausa Society and Culture—Stories: There is an extensive oral literature in Hausa of folk tales and proverbs. Some of this has come to be written down in colloquial Hausa. Perhaps the best example of such stories is *Magana jari ce (Discussion is an Asset)*, a three-volume work by Abubakar Imam. Contained in the volumes are several dozen short stories, each based on a Hausa proverb. One of the stories, for example, is based on the proverb "manafunci dodo ya kan ci mai shi" ("treachery is an evil spirit who returns to kill its owner"). The story concerns a young prince who saves the life of a poor and abandoned child. The child, in turn, grows up and through a series of deceptions and intrigues, betrays the prince for his own gain. The treachery eventually becomes known and the man is put to death. The beauty of the *Magana jari ce* stories lies partly in the rich vocabulary, drama, and humor employed by the author, and partly in the moral instruction of the stories. The stories are widely known throughout northern Nigeria, and the published volumes are used as Hausa literature textbooks at all school levels.

Hausa Society and Culture—Religion: Religious writings in Hausa constitute perhaps the largest single category of Hausa literature. Many of the works of the early nineteenth-century Fulani leaders, such as Usman dan Fodio, his brother Abdullahi, and his son Muhammad Bello, were written in Hausa or have subsequently been translated into Hausa from Arabic and/or Fulani. There are a number of contemporary writers who deal with the themes of morality and law, God and theology, or Islamic history. Haliru Binji, who was formerly Deputy Grand Qadi in Northern Nigeria, has been a leader in the effort to interpret Islamic traditions in a modern context. The writings of Abubakar Imam provide a concise introduction to Islamic requirements. Younger men, such as Sheikh Ahmed Lemu, have London degrees in Arabic and are essentially teachers engaged in secondary or college-level education.

As with religious poetry, to be discussed later, many writers select topics related to the Islamic brotherhoods in northern Nigeria (especially the Tijaniyya and Qadiriyya).

Hausa History: A number of contemporary scholars in northern Nigeria have written historical essays in Hausa. The Waziri of Sokoto, M. Junaidu, discusses the history of the Fulani in West Africa in *Tarihin Fulani*. The Waziri of Kano, M. Abubakar Dokaji, has written a history of Kano from earliest times called *Kano ta Dabo Cigari,* drawing both on manuscripts and on oral tradition. For the student of history, there are a large number of historical documents in Hausa in the National Archives, Kaduna, and in the private collections of religious mallams. In addition, there exist a number of biographies in Hausa, both "official" and "unofficial," which are relevant to historical studies, such as the biography of the late Emir of Kano, Abdullahi Bayero.

Social Change: During the 1950s the adult literacy campaign in Northern Nigeria produced a number of books dealing with modern techniques of farming, health, marketing, etc. In the independence era, the Ministry of Information and Public Enlightenment has coordinated publications of this same sort. Also, school textbooks have been generated which deal with modern subjects. One example is *Ikon Allah (The Power of God)*, which is full-sized textbook on natural sciences.

In addition, there are anthologies of articles or special features from the major Hausa newspaper — *Gaskiya ta ki kwabo (Truth Is Worth More Than a Penny)*. Such works constitute a distinct body of literature, which seems to be related to the general processes of social change.

Hausa Political Literature: Many of the writings of Alhaji Aminu Kano, former leader of the opposition party in Northern Nigeria, and present Federal Commissioner of Communications, are untranslated. One of the more fundamental works is his autobiographical account of his education and travels in Europe (entitled *Motsi ya fi zama*). The biography of Aminu Kano by Lawan Danbazau is also significant. More recently, some of the Kano state literature (such as *Kano State, Jiya da Yau*) is available only in Hausa.

Much of the Hausa political literature is in the form of poetry. The writings of Sa'adu Zungur, and literally dozens of other writers in the 1950s, focused on issues of fundamental political importance. Zungur was a graduate of Yaba College, Lagos, and was one of the founders of NEPU (Northern Elements Progressive Union). In a poem entitled *Arewa, Junhuria ko mulukiya (The North, Democracy or Monarchy)* Zungur identified many of the problems of post-colonial "democracy" in Nigeria. At the same time, he warned the Emirs to reform and to institute justice. Most of the writings of the late Ahmadu Bello are in English, although a Hausa version of his full-length autobiography does exist (entitled *Rayuwata*).

Contemporary Hausa Literature and Poetry: The literature and poetry of contemporary northern Nigeria may be divided into the secular and the religious. Secular poets, including Naibi Wali, Salihu Kwantagora, Mu'azu Hadeja, Sa'adu Zungur, and Mudi Sipikin, have focused on a range of topics, from morals to everyday life to politics. (It should be noted that poetry focusing on "romantic love" is almost nonexistent.) Almost all of the secular poets have two things in common: some Western education and training in Arabic.

Poets focusing on religious themes have been a part of Hausa and Fulani culture for many centuries. At present, there are poets such as Aliyu na-Mangi of Zaria whose work (see *Wakar Infiraji*) covers every aspect of moral and spiritual life. There are also poets whose writings focus on their own particular "denomination" (i.e., sufi brotherhood, or *tarika*). Much of this writing is mystical and highly personal.

In other forms, such as the novel, the short story, and the play, there is a considerable amount of experimentation at present, although all writers draw heavily on the Hausa-Fulani culture.

SELECTED WORKS IN HAUSA

I. Society and Culture

A. Stories and Tales

Ahmad, Baba
Ban dariya (Funny Stories)
Zaria: NORLA, Gaskiya Corporation, 1st ed. 1954; 2d ed. 1958.
    Traditional amusing stories of Mallams, in the Hausa context.

Anon.
Karin magana (Proverbs)
Zaria: NORLA, Gaskiya Corporation, 1957.
    Traditional Hausa proverbs.

Anon.
Idon matambayi (The Eye of the Questioner)
Zaria: NORLA, Gaskiya Corporation, 1955.
    Adventure story in a traditional setting.

Anon.
Labaru na da da na yanzu (Stories of Past and Present)
Zaria: Gaskiya Corporation, 1968.
    Traditional stories collected from many sources, folk tales, riddles, proverbs and moral teaching, etc.

Anon.
Labarin Tanimuddari (The Story of Tanimuddari)
Zaria: NORLA, Gaskiya Corporation, 1958.
    A traditional story adapted to Hausa culture from a Middle Eastern adventure story.

Balewa, Abubakar Tafawa
Shaihu Umar
Zaria: NORLA, Gaskiya Corporation, 1955.
    A traditional Hausa story in novelette form. Deals with the adventures of Shaihu Umar during the time of slave trade. The author, former Prime Minister of the Federation of Nigeria, is now deceased.

Gamagira, Sa'idu
Littafin mafarki (Dream Book)
Zaria: Gaskiya Corporation, 1963.
    Dreams interpreted within a Hausa cultural context.

Imam, Abubakar

Magana jari ce (Discussion is an Asset)
Zaria: NORLA, Gaskiya Corporation, 1939; reprinted 1954.
> A three-volume collection of stories. The stories have been taken from all over the world, put into the Hausa context and translated and rewritten by Abubakar Imam. The stories are built on Hausa proverbs and portray the culture of the Hausa people.

Kano, Mamman
Dare dubu da daya (A Thousand and One Nights)
Zaria: Gaskiya Corporation, 1961.
> Stories of the Arabian Nights translated into Hausa.

Kumasi, Muhammadu Muntaka
Littafin mamaki (Book of Wonder)
Zaria: Gaskiya Corporation, 1963.
> Traditional stories of events which happened in the Middle East to Hausa pagans (Bamaguje).

Mairiga, Usuman
Iblis Dan Lis (Satan)
Zaria: Gaskiya Corporation, 1959.
> Traditional stories of Satan, his evil tricks and his followers.

Mani, Abdulmalik
Bayan wuya sai dadi (After Difficulty, Only Comfort)
Zaria: NORLA, Gaskiya Corporation, 1954.
> A traditional story describing the travels and adventures of Tuareg traders.

Zango, Tanko
Da'u Fataken Dare (Da'u, Merchant of the Night)
Zaria: Gaskiya Corporation, n.d. (Vol. IV of the *littattafan hira* series).
> Three traditional stories of Hausa thieves, or "Merchants of the Night," of whom the greatest was Da'u.

B. Religious Life

Abubakar, Sultan of Sokoto
Hali zanen dutse (Habit Is an Inscription in Stone)
Zaria: NORLA, Gaskiya Corporation, 1954.
> Homily on obligations to parents, the good and moral life, food, prayers, virtues, etc.

Ahmad, Baba
Masu hikima sun ce (The Possessors of Wisdom Have Said)
Zaria: NORLA, Gaskiya Corporation, 1955.
> Religious instruction giving rules, prohibitions, dogmas and moral teachings.

Ahmed, M. K.
Aikin Hajji a saukake (The Pilgrimage Made Easy)
Zaria: Gaskiya Corporation, 1967.
  Religious instruction providing a travel guide for Nigerian pilgrims to Mecca.

Al-Kirawani, Abdullahi Ibn Abi Zaid
Risala
Zaria: Gaskiya Corporation, n.d.
  Commentary on Maliki law: The standard textbook on Maliki law in Nigeria, written in the eleventh century in North Africa. This version is written in Arabic but explained in Hausa.

Anon.
Manhajar ilmin addinin Musulunci (A Syllabus of Muslim Religion)
Zaria: NORLA, 1958. (Hausa and Arabic)
  Religious instruction for children including a planned program of Koranic instruction weekly giving references from the Koran and other published works.

Anon.
Zuhudu (Mysticism)
Zaria: NORLA, Gaskiya Corporation, 1955 (Ajami script).
  Religious poetry preaching rejection of this world and love of the next world.

Anon.
Tauhidi a saukake (The Doctrine of Divine Unity Made Easy)
Zaria: Gaskiya Corporation, n.d. (Ajami script).
  Theological instruction and explanation of the unity of God.

Azare, Garba Affa
Wakar tauhidi da salla (A Poem on Divine Unity and Prayer)
Zaria: NORLA, Gaskiya Corporation, 1958.
  Religious poetry giving a series of prayers for various occasions.

Bakurdabe, Yahaya
Alkurlabi
Zaria: Gaskiya Corporation, 1959 (Bilingual: Hausa boko and Arabic).
  Religious instruction explaining the five pillars of Islam.

Binji, Haliru
Littafin Addini (Book of Religion)
Zaria: NORLA, Gaskiya Corporation, 1959.
  Religious instruction including a review of obligations, doctrines, history, etc.

Binji, Haliru

Ibada da hukunci (Worship and Authority)
Zaria: Gaskiya Corporation, 1960.
> Commentary on Maliki law. Gives specific information on fasting, taxes, gifts, Jihad, etc.

dan Almajiri, Muhammad (of Kano)
Tsarabar iyali (Provisions for Family)
Kano: Northern Maktabat Printing Press, 1960 (Ajami script).
> Jurisprudence regarding family matters. Also prayers are discussed.

dan Fodio, Abdullah
Hasken mahukumta (The Light of the Rulers)
Zaria: Gaskiya Corporation, 1968.
> General instruction on Islamic laws, including criminal procedures, holy war, inheritance, etc.

dan Fodio, Usman
Shika-shikan walitaka (The Pillars of Sainthood)
Zaria: Gaskiya Corporation, n.d. (Bilingual: Hausa boko and Arabic).
> Leader of Jihad discusses origins of sainthood, magic, blessing, and other aspects of the Sufi tradition.

Mani, Usman
Alhajjul Mabrur
Zaria: Gaskiya Corporation, 1959.
> Religious instruction for pilgrimage to Mecca. Questions and answers for pilgrims regarding the holy places. Book also mentions modern ways of transporting pilgrims.

Zaria, Shu'aibu Usman
Addini a saukake (Religion with Ease)
Zaria: NORLA, Gaskiya Corporation, 1956 (Ajami script).
> General religious instruction.

Zariya, Muhammadu Muntaka
Duniya ina gabanki (World, Where Is Your Front Side)
Zaria: NORLA, Gaskiya Corporation, n.d.
> Religious instruction: A description of some events from a traditional religious viewpoint.

Zariya, Umar Ibrahim (Alkalin Zazzau)
Mulkin Halifa Umar (The Government of Caliph Umar)
Zaria: NORLA, Gaskiya Corporation, 1954.
> Religious and legal instruction including a commentary on the legal obligations and responsibilities of government derived from the period of Caliph Umar, with some sayings from the Caliph.

II. History

Anon.
Kafawar mulki Fulani a kasar Kwantagoro (Fulani Rule in Kontagoro)
Zaria: Gaskiya Corporation, 1968.
> A history of Kontagoro from 1736 until the coming of the British. The account deals with local wars and chiefs.

Anon.
Wali Dammarina na birnin Katsina (Saint Dammarina of Katsina City)
Zaria: NORLA, Gaskiya Corporation, 1954.
> The story of a religious personage in Katsina.

Anon.
Amina Sarauniyar Zazzau (Amina, Queen of Zaria)
Zaria: NORLA, Gaskiya Corporation, 1954.
> A prose history account of the Queen of Zaria, Amina, who reigned during the sixteenth century.

Anon.
Sarkin Kano, Alhaji Abdullahi Bayero C.M.G., C.B.E. (The Emir of Kano Alhaji Abdullahi Bayero C.M.G., C.B.E.)
Zaria: NORLA, Gaskiya Corporation, 1954.
> The official biography of the Emir of Kano, Alhaji Abdullahi Bayero (1884–1954).

Bamalli, Nuhu
Abdulkadir Saladin
Zaria: Gaskiya Corporation, 1951.
> A historical novel of the adventures of Saladin Pasha during the period 1880–1900 with the Mahdi of the Sudan, Muhammed Ahmed.

dan Fodio, Usman
Littattafai uku a hade (Three Books Combined)
Zaria: Gaskiya Corporation, n.d. (Bilingual: Hausa and Arabic).
> Three works written by the Jihad leader on various aspects of Islamic religion.

dan Fodio, Usman
Ma'a Ma'are
Zaria: NORLA, Gaskiya Corporation, 1955 (Ajami script).
> Religious poetry originally written in Fulani by Shehu Usman, translated into Hausa by his son, Isa.

Gambarawa, Mustafa (Katsina)
Rabon gado (Dividing Inheritance)
Zaria: NORLA, Gaskiya Corporation, 1959.

A commentary on Maliki law, giving a minute description of inheritance sharing according to a variety of situations and types of property.

Gumi, Abubakar Mahmud
Hadisai arba'in (Forty Hadiths)
Zaria: NORLA, Gaskiya Corporation, 1959 (Bilingual: Hausa and Arabic).
   Religious instruction giving traditions concerning the Prophet Muhammad.

Idris, Sheikh Tayyib
Jagorar mai salla (A Guide to He Who Prays)
London: Evans Bros., n.d. (Boko and ajami script).
   Religious instructions for proper prostrations, washings, etc.

Imam, Abubakar
Musulunci I (A First Book on the Muslim Religion)
Zaria: Gaskiya Corporation, 1960.
   Introductory work on law, prayers, fasting, the life of Muhammad. Quotations from the Holy Koran are in Arabic.

Imam, Abubakar
Hajji mabudin ilmi (The Pilgrim Is the Key to Knowledge)
Zaria: NORLA, Gaskiya Corporation, 1954.
   A series of questions and answers concerning the pilgrimage to Mecca; obligations and customs, etc.

Kano, Saminu Sa'd 'Yantandu
Hisabi asawwake (Easy Method of Learning Hisabi)
Kano: Native Authority Press, n.d.
   Hisabi (astrology) is complex in Hausa society. The author provides a guide to the numerological basis of astrology.

Lemu, Skeikh Ahmed
Sakon Malam (The Teacher's Message)
Zaria: Gaskiya Corporation, 1968 (Ajami script)
   Religious instructions on the existence of God, the next world, the Prophet Muhammad, the Koran, etc.

Bamalli, Nuhu
Mungo Park. Mabudin Kwara (Mungo Park. Key to the Niger River)
Zaria: Gaskiya Corporation, 1955.
   Translated accounts of Mungo Park's first and second travels along the River Niger.

Bello (Walin Katsina)
Gandoki ("Overexcitable")
Zaria: NORLA, Gaskiya Corporation, 1934.
   Historical fiction of the Kontagora wars with the invading British.

Buhari, Muhammadu
Salsalar Ahmadu Bello, Firimiyan Jihar Arewa (The Spiritual Lineage of Ahmadu Bello, the Premier of the North)
Zaria: Gaskiya Corporation, n.d. (Bilingual: Hausa ajami and Arabic)
   The spiritual lineage of Ahmadu Bello, written in poetic form.

Dokaji, Abubakar
Kano ta Dabo Cigari (The Kano of Dabo Cigari)
Zaria: Gaskiya Corporation, 1959.
   An authoritative history of Kano City from its founding to modern times. Author is the Waziri of Kano.

Ilorin, Sule
Tarihin goro (The History of Cola Nuts)
Zaria: NORLA, Gaskiya Corporation, 1958.
   A discussion of the history of cola nuts and of Hausa merchant trading in cola nuts; an interpretation as to why Hausa people are such large consumers of cola nuts.

Imam, Abubakar
Hausa bakwai (The Seven Hausa States)
Zaria: NORLA, Gaskiya Corporation, 1954.
   Traditional history of the origins of Hausa states beginning with Daura.

Imam, Abubakar
Sayyadina Abubakar (The Noble Abubakar)
Zaria: NORLA, Gaskiya Corporation, 1954.
   A religious history of the first Caliph Abubakar and his times.

Imam, Abubakar
Tarihin Annabi (History of the Prophet)
Zaria: NORLA, Gaskiya Corporation, n.d. (written after 1954), three volumes.
   Religious and instructive biography; gives a history of the life, work, sayings, and importance of the Prophet Muhammad. Also contains a biography of the author and some of his poems.

Jangari Cultural Organization
Kano State jiya da yau AD 999. 1864–1968 (Kano State Yesterday and Today AD 999. 1864–1968)
Zaria: Gaskiya Corporation, 1968.
   The history of the last battles of Kano and short biographies of successful business men of Kano (23 photos).

Jirgi, Dan Galadiman Hadeja
Sarkin Arewan Hadeja, Tatagana (The Chief of Northern Hadeja, Tatagana)
Zaria: Gaskiya Corporation, 1955.

Biography of Hadeja Chief Tatagana, including his battles and how he was assassinated.

Janaidu, Wazirin Sokoto
Hubbaren· Mujaddidi Shehu Usmanu dan-Fodiyo (The Tomb of Reformer Shaikh Usman dan Fodio)
Zaria: Gaskiya Corporation, 1961 (Boko and ajami script)
   Guide to the tomb of Shehu Usman.

Janaidu, Wazirin Sokoto
Tarihin Fulani (History of the Fulani)
Zaria: NORLA, Gaskiya Corporation, 1957.
   Prose history of the Toronkawa Fulani. Traces the Toronkawa from the Senegal valley to Northern Nigeria. Draws upon oral traditions concerning the Jihad, founding of Sokoto, and nineteenth-century wars and personalities.

Kankiya, Malam Mani
Dammaliki a birnin Katsina aka yi shi (Dammaliki was Created in Katsina City)
Zaria: NORLA, Gaskiya Corporation, 1955.
   Traditional story regarding the times when Katsina was subject to Sokoto and a notorious viceroy called Damaliki who reigned there.

Mai Maina, Muhammadu
Maimaina: Sarkin Askira (The Autobiography of Mai Maina)
Zaria: NORLA, Gaskiya Corporation, 1958.
   The autobiography of a spy and mercenary soldier for the British during the establishment of the Protectorate in Northern Nigeria.

Mairiga, Malam Usuman
Sayyadina Usuman
Zaria: Gaskiya Corporation, 1960.
   A biography of the Third Caliph Usman.

Mani, Abdulmalik
Zuwan Turawa Nijeriya ta Arewa (The Coming of the Europeans to Northern Nigeria)
London: NORLA, Longmans, Green, 1957.
   A prose history description of the arrival of Europeans, in Northern Nigeria, from early slavers to Lugard, making use of local traditions and European sources. Also covers several Emirates specifically: Kano, Hadejia, Zaria, Katsina, Abuja, Bornu, and Sokoto.

Nunku, Adamu
Tarihin Mada (The History of Mada)
Zaria: NORLA, Gaskiya Corporation, 1955.
   A traditional history of the Mada people, who inhabit the lands south of Jos.

Tureta, Abdulbaki
Abdulbaki
Zaria: NORLA, Gaskiya Corporation, 1954.
An autobiography which provides information concerning events in Sokoto during pre-colonial times. Abdulbaki was the son of the District Head of Tureta in Sokoto. He was originally a slave.

III. Social Change

Anon.
Gyada da shukar taba (Groundnuts and Tobacco Growing)
Zaria: NORLA, Gaskiya Corporation, 1955.
Agricultural information concerning the planting and cultivation of tobacco and groundnuts.

Anon.
Hanyar lissafi (The Way of Arithmetic)
Zaria: Gaskiya Corporation, 1966.
An adult education primer in arithmetic regarding the uses of numbers, weights, liquids, money, and distance.

Anon.
Girke-Girke (Cooking)
Zaria: NORLA, Gaskiya Corporation, 1955.
Health and housekeeping instructions on how to prepare and cook food in a sanitary manner.

Auna, Yacubu
Itacen wuta da na aikace-aikace (Firewood and Timber)
Zaria: Gaskiya Corporation, n.d.
Conservation literature: two articles on the need for and techniques of soil and tree conservation.

Bamalli, Nuhu
Bala da babiya (Bala and Babiya)
Zaria: Gaskiya Corporation, 1968.
Health science: an account of a sanitary inspector and his wife and the way they changed the attitudes of a whole village toward cleanliness.

East, Rupert, and Imam, Abubakar
Ikon Allah (The Power of God)
Zaria: NORLA, Gaskiya Corporation, 1954.
Instruction in natural sciences: elementary discussions of physical science, air, water, land, and astronomy.

Ingawa, Ahmadu
Zaman mutun da sana'arsa (Man's Living and Occupations)

Zaria: Gaskiya Corporation, 1963.
   Descriptions of the occupations of man.

Nigerian Citizen
Sauna Jac (Foolish Jac)
Zaria: NORLA, Gaskiya Corporation, n.d.
   Cartoons taken from *The Nigerian Citizen*. Picaro-type adventures of a prima-
   ry school-leaver in Hausaland, illustrating relations with Europeans, market
   situations, etc.

Zariya, Nuhu
Ashe ana cin waken soya? (Really, Are Soybeans Eaten?)
Zaria: Gaskiya Corporation, n.d.
   Agricultural development propaganda: describes the origin, uses, and pro-
   duction of soybeans.

Zariya, Nuhu
Riyiya gidan ruwa (A Well: The House of Water)
Zaria: Gaskiya Corporation, 1955.
   Propaganda on sanitation. How to take care of wells and prevent the con-
   tamination of water.

IV. Nation-Building

Anon.
Firimiyan jihar Arewa na Farko . . . Ahmadu Bello (The First Premier of the North-
ern Region . . . Ahmadu Bello)
Zaria: NORLA, Gaskiya Corporation, 1956.
   Biography of Ahmadu Bello, complete with photographs.

Bello, Sir Ahmadu
Rayuwata (My Life)
Zaria: Gaskiya Corporation, 1961.
   Descriptive autobiography of late Premier of Northern Region. Gives in-
   terpretation of Nigerian history, the Fulani and the independence move-
   ment, maps, genealogies.

Danbazau, Lawan
Aminu Kano
Zaria: Gaskiya Corporation, 1963.
   Biography of Aminu Kano, leader of the banned political party NEPU, and
   now Nigerian Federal Commissioner.

Kano, Aminu
Motsi sa fi zama (Moving Surpasses Sitting)
Zaria: NORLA, Gaskiya Corporation, 1955.
   A description by Aminu Kano of his European educational experience.

Parsons, F. W.
Dokar Hanyar tafiyad da huknuncin laifi (Rules for the Prosecution of Law Breakers)
Kaduna: Government Printer, 1960.
> The Hausa version of the criminal procedure code of Northern Nigeria, 1960.

V. Contemporary Literature

Abdullah, Jahiru
Nagari na kowa (Quality is For All)
Zaria: Gaskiya Corporation, 1968.
> A story of poor parents forced to abandon their son who later became a chief through his own efforts.

Anon.
Wakokin Hausa (Hausa Poems)
Zaria: NORLA, Gaskiya Corporation, 1957.
> Selections of Hausa poems by well-known Hausa poets, including younger contemporary writers.

Daura, Sa'idu Ahmed
Tauraruwar hamada (The Desert Star)
Zaria: Gaskiya Corporation, 1959.
> A novel about a beautiful girl who was the cause of battles and adventures between her suitors.

Hadeja, Mu'azu
Wakokin Ma'azu Hadeja (Mu'azu Hadeja's Poems)
Zaria: Gaskiya Corporation, 1967.
> Ten poems, most of which appeal to the Hausa people to wake up and participate in the modern world.

Imam, Abubakar
Ruwan Bagaja (The Water of Bagaja)
Zaria: Gaskiya Corporation, 1968.
> The title is derived from the name of a folk tale. The first-person novel relates the adventures of Alhaji Imam in finding the magic water. The story resembles the adventures of Aladdin in Arabic literature.

Kano, Dauda
Tabarmar kunya (The Mat of Shame)
Zaria: Gaskiya Corporation, 1969.
> A Hausa comedy play portraying a son-in-law who inadvertently goes to the bedroom of his parents-in-law at night, and, thinking he is talking to his wife, "tells all."

Kontagora, Salihu
Gaskiya maidaci (Truth Is Bitter)
Zaria: NORLA, Gaskiya Corporation, 1955 (Ajami script).
   Poetry by a well-known contemporary writer who appeals to people to tell
   the truth.

Makarfi, Shu'aibu
Jatau na Kyallu (Jatau of Kyallu)
Zaria: Gaskiya Corporation, 1960.
   A play portraying relationships in Hausa society when a wealthy man mar-
   ries a professional prostitute. She isolates him from his friends, relatives, and
   other wives, and causes the loss of his money. She reduces him to a state of
   chaos.

Makarfi, Shu'aibu
Zamanin nan namu (This Time of Ours)
Zaria: NORLA, Gaskiya Corporation, 1959.
   Two plays portraying traditional Hausa life, customs, and humor—especially
   the role of the Mallams.

Na-mangi, Aliyu (of Zaria)
Wakar Imfiraji (A Poem of God)
Zaria: Gaskiya Corporation, n.d. (There were 8 volumes in all published from
1959 to 1961. They are available in both ajami and boko script.)
   This blind, elderly poet is one of the most famous traditional poets in
   northern Nigeria. His poems cover all aspects of life from a religious point
   of view.

Zungur, Sa'adu
Wakokin M. Sa'adu Zungur (The Poetry of M. Sa'adu Zungur)
Zaria: Gaskiya Corporation, 1968, 2nd ed.
   The author was a leading figure in the Northern Elements Progressive
   Union before his death in the late 1950s. His poetry is regarded as among
   the best of "modern" literature. He deals with issues of innovation, return-
   ing soldiers, democracy vs. kingship, etc.

SWAHILI LITERATURE

The oldest known Swahili manuscript dates from 1728,[1] but the literary
tradition of which it is a part is undoubtedly much older. Until the twentieth
century, written (as opposed to oral or folk) literature, which used the Arabic

1. Lyndon Harries, *Swahili Poetry* (London: Oxford University Press, 1962), p. 5.

script, was confined almost exclusively to verse. However, a number of prose chronicles of some of the important or once-important Swahili cities (such as Kilwa, Pate, Lamu, and Mombasa) were written down in Swahili at least as early as the nineteenth century.[2] Traditional Swahili poetry follows strict canons of rhyme and meter, inspired by the example of Arabic, which also serves as the source for much of its subject matter. However, what is regarded by many as the greatest traditional Swahili poem, the *utenzi* or epic of Liongo Fumo, is entirely East African in content and setting. Furthermore, in later years poems were written about local historical events, such as the Maji Maji rebellion of 1905 against German rule in Tanganyika.

The language of the traditional poetry is very difficult for most speakers of contemporary Swahili—in some cases as difficult as is the language of Chaucer for speakers of present-day English. One reason for this is that words are borrowed freely from Arabic, and these are not a part of the normal vocabulary. Many archaic words and forms are used, sometimes referred to as *kingozi* (archaic language). Finally, the grammar and pronunciation derive not from the dialect of Zanzibar, on which the modern standard is based, but from that of Lamu on the northern Kenya coast, which was the center of the earlier literary tradition.

An idiom much closer to the modern standard, yet retaining the traditional patterns of rhyme and meter, has been adopted by most poets of recent decades, including the late Shaaban Robert, whom many consider the greatest of twentieth-century Swahili writers. During this same period, Swahili has been put to many new uses, both utilitarian (newspapers and textbooks) and literary (novels and plays). Among the latter, probably the most famous is the translation of Shakespeare's *Julius Caesar* by Julius Nyerere, president of Tanzania. Other imaginative writers have added new genres—for example, Muhammad Said Abdulla, whose mystery novel *Mzimu wa watu wa kale* won wide admiration. Now that Swahili has achieved the status of national language in Tanzania, there is every reason to expect an increasingly flourishing literature.

SELECTED WORKS IN SWAHILI

I. Society and Culture

A. Stories and Tales

Anon.

---

2. A. H. J. Prins, "On Swahili Historiography," *Journal of the East African Swahili Committee,* July, 1958.

Hekaya za abunawas (Collections of Stories)
London: Macmillan, 1927.

Anon.
Hadithi za Esopo (Chuo cha kwanza cha kusomea) (The Stories of Esopo)
Kiungani, Zanzibar: Mission Press, 1895.
    This book is a classic of old East African tales.

Diva, D. E.
Sungura mjanja (A Hare Is a Rascal)
Nairobi: Eagle Press, 1953.
    Traditional tales for children and adults.

Farsi, Sheikh S. S.
Swahili Sayings fröm Zanzibar
Dar es Salaam: Eagle Press, 1953.
    Book 1, *Methali* (Proverbs); Book 2, *Vitendawili na imani za ushirikina* (Riddles
    and Superstitions).

Meena, E. K.; Mmari, G. V. ; and Sangiwa, H. H.
Vitendawili (Swahili Riddles)
Nairobi: Oxford University Press, 1960.
    Idiomatic expressions from different tribes in Tanganyika.

Mnyampala, Mathias E.
Kisa cha mrina asali na wenzake Wawili (Tales of Tanganyika, Book 2)
Dar es Salaam: East African Literature Bureau, 1966.
    The adventures of a honey-gatherer and his two friends.

Moore, Adrienne
Hadithi za Kikwetu: Hadithi za kaka fisi (Traditional African Stories, Book 1:
Stories about Hyenas)
Nairobi: East African Publishing House, 1967.

Sheiza, Otto Anthony
Asili ya chumvi ya bahari (The Origin of Sea Salt and Other Sambaa Stories)

B. Particular Customs

Farsy, Shekh Muhammad Saleh Abdallah
Ada za Harusi katika unguja (Marriage Customs in Zanzibar)
Dar es Salaam: East African Literature Bureau, 1965.

Hadumbavhinu, L.
Waluguru na desturi zao (Customs and Traditions of the Waluguru)
Dar es Salaam: East African Literature Bureau, 1968.
    A collection of useful information on customs and traditions of the Walu-
    guru of Tanzania.

Harries, Lyndon (trans.)
Utenzi wa mkunumbi (Johari za Kiswahili series, no. 8)
Dar es Salaam: East African Literature Bureau, 1967.
An account of a Swahili potlatch. The original Arabic script on which the text is based has been carefully calligraphed and reproduced in this book.

Thonya, Lucius M.
Siasa hapo kale (Political Wisdom of the Past among the Angoni)

Kombo, Salum
Ustaarabu na maendeleo ya Mwafrika (Civilization and Progress of the African People)
Nairobi: East African Literature Bureau, 1966.

Mochiwa, A.
Habari za Wazigua (Customs of the Wazigua People of Tanzania)

Ngala, R. G.
Nchi na desturi za Wagiriama (The Land and Culture of the Wagiriama)
Nairobi: Eagle Press, 1949.
A description of an East African culture.

Ntiro, S. J.
Desturi za Wachagga (Customs and Traditions of the Chagga People of Tanzania.

Otiende, J. D.
Habari za Abaluyia (The Customs and Traditions of the Abaluyia)
Nairobi: Eagle Press, 1949.
The traditional customs of the Abaluyia people of Nyanza Province, Kenya.

Velten, C.
Desturi za Wasuaheli na Khabari za desturi za sheria za Wasuaheli ((The Habits and Norms of the Swahili People)
Göttingen: Dandenhoed & Ruprecht, 1903.
This deals with traditional Swahili cultural characteristics before colonization.

II. History

Abdallah, Hemed
Utenzi wa Seyyidna Husein bin Ali (Johari za Kiswahili series, no. 6) (The History of Prince Hussein, Son of Ali)
Dar es Salaam: East African Literature Bureau, 1965.

Chacha, G. N.
Historia ya Abakuria na sheria zao (The History of the Abakuria and their Customs)

Chum, Haji
Utenzi wa vita vya Uhud (Johari za Kiswahili series, no. 3) (The Epic of the Battle of Uhud)
Dar es Salaam: East African Literature Bureau, 1962.
   Traditional Arabic poems, passed on orally from generation to generation and eventually written in Swahili.

Hemedi bin Abdallah bin Said bin Masudi el Buhriy (trans. J. W. T. Allen)
Utenzi wa vita vya Wadachi Kutamalaki Mrima 1307 A. H. (Johari za Kiswahili series, no. 1) (The German Conquest of the Swahili Coast)
Nairobi: East African Literature Bureau, 2d ed., 1960.

Hemedi, Ramadhani Mzee
Mapokeo ya historia ya Wairaqw (The History of the Iraqw People)

Kabeya, Rev. Father J.
Mtemi mirambo: Watu mashuhuri wa Tanzania (Famous Men of Tanzania)

Kayamba, H. T.
Tulivyoona na tulivyofanya Uingereza (What We Saw and What We Did in England)
London: Sheldon Press, 1932.

Lemenye, Justin
Maishi ya Sumeni Ole Kivasis yaani Justin Lemenye (The Life of Justin Lemenye)

Masuha, John M.
Masimulizi juu ya Wasukuma (History, Customs, and Traditions of the Sukuma of Tanzania)
Dar es Salaam, Kampala, Nairobi: Eagle Press, 1956.

Mbotela, J.
Uhuru wa watumwa (The Freedom of Slaves)
London: Sheldon Press, 1934; New York: Thomas Nelson, 1959.
   An African's perspective in his quest to gain freedom from slavery.

Mnyampala, Mathias E.
Historia, Mila na desturi za Wagogo wa Tanganyika (History and Customs of the Wagogo of Tanganyika)

Omar, Shariff C. A.
Kisiwa cha Pemba: Historia na masimulizi (History and Traditions of the Island of Pemba)

III. Social Change

Hughes, G.
Miti ni mali (Trees Are Wealth)

Hughes, G.
Ngombe ni mali (Cattle Are Wealth)

Hughes, G.
Maji ni mali (Water Is Wealth)

Humphrey, N.
Mali ya Waafrika ni nini? (What Is Africa's Wealth?)

Koeune, Esther, and Twining, H. M.
Mama wa Afrika na nyumba yake (The African Housewife and Her Home)
Kampala: Eagle Press, 1957.
   Book 1, *Nyumba* (The House and Home Nursing); Book 2, *Jiko* (The Kitch-
   en); Book 3, *Upishi* (Cookery); Book 4, *Uwanja* (The Compound); Book 5,
   Utunzaji wa nyumba (Cleaning and Care of the Home); Book 6, *Mapambo*
   (Decorating and Furnishing); Book 7, *Utunzaji wa mtoto na uuguzaji wa
   nyumbani* (Child Welfare and Home Nursing).

Mwang, John
Kushirikiana husaidia biashara (Cooperation Is a Help to Trading)

Somba, John Ndeti
Kuishi kwingi ni kuona mengi (To Live Long Is to Experience Many Events)
Nairobi: East African Publishing House, 1968.
   Stories depicting life experiences as they change from old to new.

Tanzania, Ministry of Education
Zamani mpaka siku hizi (From the Past to Today)
Dar es Salaam: Government Printer.

Twining, H. M.; Koeune, Esther; and Elliot, E. M.
Uugazaji wa nyumbani na ustawi wa watoto: Kitabu cha tatu cha msalaba mwekunda
(Home Nursing and Child Welfare Practical Booklet #3)
Dar es Salaam, Kampala, Nairobi: Eagle Press, 1956.

UNESCO
Kusoma na kuandika na maazimio na mapendekezo ya UNESCO
   Literacy as a factor in development.

IV. Nation-Building

Barongo, E. B.
Mkiki mkiki wa siasa Tanganyika (The Political Struggle for Independence in
Tanganyika)
Nairobi: East African Literature Bureau, 1966.

Kariuki, J. M.
Mau Mau kizuizini (Mau Mau Detainee)

Nairobi: East African Publishing House, 1965.

 The author spent seven years in fourteen different detention camps during the Kenya Emergency. He describes his experiences during this time, telling of torture and kindness, hunger and beatings. It is a tale of endurance, told with understanding and humility.

Kenyatta, Jomo

Ujamaa wa Kiafrika (African Socialism)

Nairobi: East African Publishing House, 1965.

 President Jomo Kenyatta outlines the African policy toward socialism and what Kenya as a republic wishes to achieve.

Kenyatta, Jomo

Naushangilia mlima ya Kenya (Facing Mount Kenya)

Nairobi: East African Publishing House, 1966.

 Attacks European prejudices and colonialism through a skillful analysis of the customs and life of his people, the Kikuyu.

Mboya, Paul

Utawala na maendeleo ya Local Government South Nyanza 1926–1957

Mboya, Tom

Uhuru ni mwanzo (Freedom Is the Beginning)

Nairobi: East African Publishing House, 1963.

 An analysis of political conflicts in Kenya. Later revised English version appeared as *Freedom and After.*

Mwanjusi, R. K.

Abeid Amani Karume

Nairobi: East African Publishing House, 1967.

 A political biography of President Abeid Amani Karume of Zanzibar, and how he led the unification of Zanzibar and Pemba toward the Republic of Tanzania.

Mwaruka, R.

Utenzi wa jamhuri ya Tanzania (The Epic of the Republic of Tanzania)

Nairobi: East African Literature Bureau, 1968.

 A long poem covering the history of Tanzania from early times to the present day.

Oyende, J. P.

Chifu hodari wa Kjafrika (The Ideal African Chief)

Dar es Salaam, Kampala, Nairobi: Eagle Press, 1954.

 Discusses the duties of an ideal African chief during the colonial era.

V. Contemporary Literature

Abdallah, Hemed

Utenzi wa Seyyidna Husein bin Ali (Johari za Kiswahili series, no. 6)
(The History of Prince Hussein, Son of Ali)
Dar es Salaam: East African Literature Bureau, 1965.

Abdulla, Muhammad Said
Mzimu wa watu wa kale (A Spirit of the Past)
Nairobi: East African Literature Bureau, 1968.
    A Swahili thriller; won first prize in the Swahili story-writing competition.

Akilimali, K. H. A.
Diwani ya Akilimali (A Book of Akilimali's Poems)
Nairobi: East African Literature Bureau, 1963.

Amri Abedi, K.
Sheria za kutunga mashairi na diwani ya Amri (The Poems of Amri, with an Essay
on Swahili Poetry and the Rules of Versification)
Kampala: Eagle Press, 1954.

Anon.
Mashairi ya Mambo Leo (Kitabu cha pili)
London: Sheldon Press, 1946.
    Contemporary poetry from the Swahili newspaper *Mambo Leo.*

Farsy, Muhammad Saleh
Kurwa na Doto
Nairobi: East African Literature Bureau, 1968.
    A novel depicting life in a typical Zanzibar village.

Kareithi, P. M.
Kaburi bila msalaba (A Grave without a Cross)
Nairobi: East African Publishing House, 1969.
    Fictional stories about the Mau Mau war.

Katalambula, Faraji
Simu ya kifo (Trail of Death)
Dar es Salaam: East African Literature Bureau, 1965.
    Contemporary fiction.

Matindi, Anne
Jua na upepo (The Sun and Wind)
Nairobi: East African Publishing House, 1968.
    Children's literature and stories.

Michuki, David N.
Mawaidha wa Wamuchuthe (The Wisdom of Wamuchuthe)
Nairobi: East African Publishing House, 1969.
    Poetry.

Mnyampala, Mathias E.

Fasili joahri ya mashairi
Dar es Salaam: The Swahili Committee of East Africa, Thakers Limited, 1964.
   A collection of poems, original in style and thought.

Mnyampala, Mathias E.
Diwani ani ya Mnyampala (A Book of Mnyampala's Poems)
Dar es Salaam: East African Literature Bureau, 1963.

Ngugi, Gerishon
Nimelogwa! Nisiwe na mpenzi (I Have Been Bewitched! I Haven't Got a Lover)
Nairobi: East African Literature Bureau, 1961.

Nyerere, Julius
Julius Caesar
Dar es Salaam, 1964
   A translation of Shakespeare.

Nkwera, F. N.
Mzishi wa baba ana radhi (Fortune Smiles on the Dutiful Child)
   A thrilling novel of a son and the reward he got from his parents. The book
   is especially recommended for its excellent use of the language.

Omolo, Leo Odera
Tajiri mjanja (Clever Wealthy Man)
Nairobi: East African Publishing House, 1967.
   Fictional stories about old-wealth Luo men.

Robert, Shaaban
Pambo la lugha (The Bantu Treasury series, Vol. XI) (Ornaments of the Language)
Johannesburg: 1947.

Robert, Shaaban
Kielezo cha insha (The Bantu Treasury series, Vol. XIII) (Model Essays)
Johannesburg: 1954.

Whiteley, W. H. (trans.)
Tippu Tip–Maishi ya Muhammed el Murjebi

Zami, J. M. S.
Mashairi yangie (My Poetry)
Kampala, Nairobi, Dar es Salaam: Eagle Press, 1953.
   The book deals with traditional East African poetry.

5

Audiovisual Aids
for African Studies

WILLIAM G. BYRNE

MOST AMERICAN COLLEGE STUDENTS have been exposed to a considerable amount of audiovisual material on Africa. This includes primarily commercial films of Europeans and their adventures in Africa: *The Snows of Kilimanjaro, The African Queen,* the *Tarzan* series, etc. More recently it includes television specials of prominent Americans, such as Jack Paar, John Glenn, or William Holden, who record with modern cameras much the same sorts of things that early European travelers did in their memoirs: the strange and exotic "native customs," the poverty, the dangers, the beauty of the physical setting. Most Western anthropologists did little to alter these stereotypes in their "ethnographical" films of African village life. There are still today hundreds of short films being distributed in Europe and America under such titles as "A Backward People: The Berbers of North Africa," "Natives of East Africa," and "Natives of Africa." Furthermore, it could probably be determined statistically from published catalogues that most of the available 16mm films about African ethnic societies focus on the Pygmies, the Bushmen, or the Watutsi, even though these groups form only a fraction of 1 per cent of the total African population.

More recently, there have been many efforts to change the focus of films about Africa. The National Educational Television (NET) films on the 1965 election in Tanzania and the apartheid situation in South Africa are remarkable both in technical terms and in the depth of understanding of African life which they exhibit. Likewise, the work of Frank Speed in Nigeria in recording traditional ceremonies before they disappear has the full support of the local people and the Nigerian government, yet at the same time accurately portrays topics which have come to be associated with "traditional" Africa. In the same way, Jean Rouch has dealt with both "traditional" and "transitional" topics in Niger Republic. Also, as mentioned in the *Syllabus* (Module 49), a number of African film-makers who are dealing with traditional and modern themes have begun to emerge on the international scene.

In the United States the new developments in educational films on Africa have been focused almost entirely at the high-school or junior-high-school level. The work of Julian Bryan is perhaps most illustrative of this direction. A selected and annotated list of films suitable for high school has been compiled by Barry Beyer.[1] As yet, no comparable list has been systematically developed for college-level African studies, although in this essay we will suggest certain films which might be used as a supplement to the *Syllabus* modules.

At the same time that new films on Africa are beginning to appear, new technical developments in audiovisual facilities are emerging which may result in an orientation away from such traditional media as 16mm films, filmstrips, tape recordings, and phonograph records. Many of these innovations come out of "educational television." We will illustrate the point with one example below.

Television is nowadays based essentially on videotape. A development of videotape, using 8.75mm motion-picture film instead of magnetic tape to record the electronic sound-and-picture images, now makes it possible to integrate all of the existing multimedia forms—films, slides, records, spoken lectures—into small, portable cartridges that can be used on relatively inexpensive equipment to play back through any television set. EVR (for "electronic video recording") is basically a playback-only system, but the costs of both playback equipment and prerecorded programs will be much lower than is possible for videotape.

It is now quite feasible to develop a series of programmed cartridges arranged to complement the modules in *The African Experience, Volume II: Syllabus.* Before considering any further details of EVR, however, it may be useful to comment on the general idea of audiovisual aids at the college level.

THE IDEA OF COLLEGE-LEVEL AUDIOVISUAL AIDS

In the literature of educational psychology it is generally agreed that graphic-verbal means of communication are better than verbal means alone, and that an appropriate film is at least equivalent to the average literature.[2] Yet at the college level it is often the preference of teachers and students not to utilize audiovisual aids. The popular opinion seems to be that college students are too old to learn much from films. Yet as early as 1928 research showed that the learning curve from films is at a peak for young people in their mid-twenties.[3]

1. Barry Beyer, *Africa South of the Sahara, A Resource and Curriculum Guide* (New York: Crowell, 1969).

2. In one case with university students, even the filmstrip method usually associated with lower schools, proved significantly superior to the lecture method. See W. H. Allen, "Audio-Visual Communication," *Encyclopedia of Educational Research* (1960), p. 115.

3. Karl U. Smith, *Cybernetic Principles of Learning and Educational Design* (Holt, Rinehart, and Winston, Inc., 1966), p. 140.

The present generation of college students represents a very sophisticated film viewing audience, many of whom have already begun to create their own films and are very capable of making insightful analysis of the media. Thus it might well be that audiovisual media as a supplement to lectures and discussions could be even more effective in college than at the lower levels. (There is some evidence that showing a film *twice* can provide an effective learning experience for students;[4] hence the popularity of short film loops in the lower levels.) Audiovisual presentations also coincide with the general pattern of cultural and professional learning by young adults in contemporary American society.

The most clear-cut principle of efficient learning confirmed by audiovisual research has to do with active student participation. Students tend to be more attentive during audiovisual stimulation, and therefore are more actively involved in learning. Participation may be of a covert nature (i.e., thinking responses) but this may be just as efficient as overt participation. The results of most research on audiovisual learning have been underrated by the fact that there are few tests as yet for nonverbal performance. At present there is no entirely satisfactory method for measuring the effectiveness of audiovisual instruction in promoting learning, problem solving, and retention.[5]

There have been notable exceptions, however, to the reluctance on the part of most college faculty to make use of audiovisual materials.[6] Indiana University has of course had a strong program using these media for many years. The Pennsylvania State University, Central Washington State College, Rensselaer Polytechnic Institute, and Stephens College have, since the early 1960s, encouraged the use and preparation of new media with some success. Also, in 1960, some of the faculty at the University of North Carolina (Chapel Hill) participated in a project using new media in several academic fields. Of the faculty participating, 74 per cent agreed that slides, motion pictures, and other audiovisual aids could be extremely effective for large-class instruction. (More recently the same techniques have been applied to small group and individual instruction as well.) More than half (53 per cent) suggested that they would like to supervise the preparation and evaluation of audiovisual material for their own classes. Approximately the same percentage noted that "suitable materials were not available for college use."[7]

A more recent study (1969) completed by Richard A. Margoles at "a large Midwestern University" reveals some further details regarding faculty objec-

    4. W. H. Allen, "Audio-Visual Communication," p. 115.

    5. Smith, *Cybernetic Principles,* p. 142.

    6. Richard Evans, *Resistance to Innovation in Higher Education,* Jossey-Bass Series in Higher Education (San Francisco State College, 1968), *passim.*

    7. James W. Brown and James W. Thornton, Jr., *New Media in Higher Education* (Association for Higher Education and the Division of Audiovisual Instruction Service of the National Educational Association, 1963), pp. 130–40.

tions to audiovisual media at the college level.[8] The most common response was that the available materials did not cover important subject matter. The least-mentioned objection was that the department was opposed or indifferent to the media. Of 70 faculty members compared for attitudes toward audiovisual usage, those with a favorable attitude most often mentioned that the faculty members generally lacked training to use the equipment. Those with unfavorable attitudes objected that "one uses too much time for the results obtained" as second on a list of thirteen objections. Faculty with favorable attitudes ranked this objection in tenth place.

Given present techniques and availability of *relevant* audiovisual materials, the mixed reactions on the part of faculty members are hardly surprising. The present techniques are cumbersome. It was revealed in the above study that the overhead projector with transparencies was many times more popular than any other type of media, probably because it is simple to operate and the image is clear. But this is really not much more sophisticated than the use of a blackboard. Movies, filmstrips, and slide shows with audio reinforcement can have a much greater impact, especially with recent improvements discussed below. Unfortunately, many of these tools are apparently too complicated to be dragged into the classroom, and, in addition, the previewing of material does take time.

As mentioned earlier in this article, many of the standard complaints about college-level audiovisual aids may be met through recent developments in videotape and film equipment. All of the present media can be integrated into one easily handled film or tape cartridge. In the summer of 1970, CBS started distributing an EVR player which operates much like a phonograph. One EVR film cartridge, with 180,000 frames, can play for fifty minutes. It needs no threading and is as easily tuned as a home TV. It can be operated at fast forward or reverse, slow scan, regular speed, or it can freeze a single frame. Any existing film, as well as any other image, can be transferred easily to the new medium. This has great potential for individual student viewing as well as for classroom use, as do the latest developments in super-8mm film loops which, though limited to shorter running times (up to twenty minutes), are nearly as versatile. These will enable the student to view individually or in a class visual presentations, moving pictures, and still shorts (e.g., maps, charts, etc.) which have been integrated with programmed instruction and reinforced with audio instruction.

Yet it will take time before sufficient materials are converted to these new forms and new material is created for instruction at the college level. Hence, it is still necessary to consider what is suitable and available, or at least adaptable, at present.

While the most fundamental objection to college-level audiovisual aids is the

8. Richard A. Margoles, "Guidelines for Implementing Media Support Service at the College Level," *Audiovisual Instruction,* November, 1969.

lack of relevant materials, there is more available than commonly supposed. Furthermore, although much of the dialogue accompanying existing films is inadequate for college audiences, this can be circumvented by the instructor's supplying his own lecture to accompany the film (i.e. by turning off the sound track). Some companies now have super-8mm projection cartridges (sometimes called film loops), filmstrip frames, and even individual 35mm slide mounts that allow an instructor to record his own information on a sound track.

With all of the above-mentioned potential improvements it is not difficult to anticipate some changes in the format of college education. In the past, most lecture presentations assumed that the student had completed the background reading assignments. It is now possible to know exactly how much of the background information has been covered by students before classroom discussion begins. If the new media with their visual impact and reinforcement do what they should do, the instructor can assume more correctly that the students *are* prepared. The lecture as a medium of communication may give way to fairly sophisticated discussions between students and teachers. The role of the professor may even change from that of disseminator of information to that of "tutor" or provocateur of dialogue.

Because of the implications of this, the newly established Center for the Teaching Professions at Northwestern University has begun focusing on the development of a media center and laboratory to make available to the faculty the latest developments in technological support for instruction and thus encourage the planning of college-level courses using a media-oriented approach.

AUDIOVISUAL AIDS AND AFRICAN STUDIES

For some purposes there is quite a bit of audio and/or visual material on Africa that may be suitable for college instruction. For other purposes and subject-matter areas there is virtually nothing. Much of what is available cannot really be judged properly from catalogue descriptions. The categories of evaluation used in most catalogues are of little value for college use. What may be judged as junior-high-school material may be adapted for college viewing, depending on the instructor. Also a visual image will mean different things to different groups. The "grading" of films by school level is based on the sound track more than anything else. If the sound track is turned off, however, the college professor can provide a suitable narrative. Dr. Paul Wendt of Southern Illinois University has explored with some success the "visual literacy" of documentary films for graduate students. Some film companies have responded to the need for updated narrative with sound and film tracks that can be erased and reworked.

Because of the confused criteria for catalogue descriptions of Africana films, Patrick O'Meara of Indiana University has suggested the following schema for film evaluation.[9]

SCHEMA FOR FILM EVALUATION

1. Story pattern (brief description of content)
2. Scene
3. Key personalities (if any)
4. Key incidents
5. Impact
   a. emotional
   b. heuristic value
6. Achievement of purposes (does it unconsciously achieve different purposes?)
7. Strengths and weaknesses
   a. clarity of purpose
   b. relevance to contemporary issues
   c. oversimplification
   d. overloading (too much information)
8. Ranges of uses

As a further point of evaluation, one might add the degree to which generalizations and concepts in the film aid a social-science perspective of the topic. Also the visual message should be clearly separated from its verbal message. Finally, while a film may fail in its stated purpose it could be valuable for other reasons. For example, the patronizing narrative of many films regarding Africans could be a useful demonstration of racial and/or ethnocentric perceptions in crosscultural research.

At this point it may be useful to mention some of the major guides to Africana audiovisual materials. Professor Daniel Crowley of the University of California at Davis has completed a census of noncommercial films on Africa which will be published shortly in the *African Studies Bulletin*. It is essentially a listing of unedited films by Africanists, with the producer's estimation of each film's value and availability. Many of these films could undoubtedly be of use to colleges and universities both in teaching and research. Such films include those by Melville Herskovits on Dahomey and Ghana, dating from 1931, as well as more recent films by anthropologists such as Merriam, Conant, Bascom, etc. Such films are historic documents in themselves, apart from their value in teaching.

9. Patrick O'Meara, "Toward a Syntax for the African Education Film," Paper delivered at the African Studies Association Annual Conference, Montreal, October, 1969.

Several institutional approaches are being made to the dissemination of information about African audiovisual materials. The Educational Materials Center of the African-American Institute (New York), although structured primarily to serve the needs of high-school systems, does keep a file on all forms of audiovisual aids in African studies, some of which might be useful at the college level. The AAI has also published a 34-page *Film Catalogue* (1968), which is available for $3.00. This catalogue is intended to emphasize "Africa today, omitting films which present the Continent and its people in a patronizing way." (The Institute also hopes to start a critical bibliography of widely used Africana teaching materials.)

In addition, the new *African Library Journal* will include a listing of new films, filmstrips, slides, and records at least once a year. It will also have a column providing guidance and suggestions on the acquisitions of Africana teaching materials, such as copies of African art objects.

The work of Barry K. Beyer (Director of Project Africa at Carnegie-Mellon University), in selecting and annotating Africana audiovisual materials for the high-school level, may also have some value at the college level. This material has been published recently as *Africa South of the Sahara, A Resource and Curriculum Guide* (New York: Crowell, 1969).

There are very few developments in Africana audiovisual evaluation that are geared specifically to college instruction. There are two projects, however, which might be of interest to the musicologist. First, Howard University has just developed a one-year course in African music for the general undergraduate student. This includes a discography of recordings, audiovisual aids, instruments, a collection of folk songs, and a syllabus. Second, Northwestern University Press is publishing Alan Merriam's *African Music on LP: An Annotated Discography*. This 200-page volume lists all commercial LP records of African music released before the end of 1965. The author has provided eighteen indexes to these recordings, including one arranged by ethnic group. Merriam does not include the International Library of African Music, Sound of Africa Series, which consists of 210 12-inch LPs. He omits these references "[because] of the detailed information available from the ILAM through its card classification system, its *Librarian's Handbook,* published in 1949 and now including updating inserts, and its catalogue."[10] For instructors not needing such a detailed study, there is the work of Klaus P. Wachsmann, *International Catalogue of Published Records of Folk Music,* (London: International Folk Music Council, 1960). Wachsmann, one of the contributors to The African Experience, Volume I: Essays, organizes his discography by country and includes brief annotations.

Merriam's work is one of five related projects sponsored by the African Studies Association. The others are the noncommercial films list by Donald Crowley (mentioned above); an inventory of privately recorded African music;

10. Alan P. Merriam, *African Music on LP: An Annotated Discography* (Evanston, Ill.: Northwestern University Press, 1970).

a survey of African visual art in American collections (work is in progress by Roy Sieber of the Department of Fine Arts, Indiana University); and, finally, a survey of commercially issued films. The latter project, based on listings in the *Educational Media Index,* was published as Occasional Paper No. 1 of the Committee of Fine Arts and the Humanities of the African Studies Association, under the title *African Film Bibliography 1965.*

Any college instructor interested in Africana films should become familiar with the work of Henry Morgenthau of National Educational Television (NET). He has written regularly in *Africa Report:* e.g., "Guide to African Films" (May, 1968), and "On Films and Film Makers" (May-June, 1969). His focus is mainly on the difficulties and recent efforts of African film-makers. Morgenthau is a leading producer of documentary films and also the husband of Ruth Schachter Morgenthau, a political scientist who has written extensively on French-speaking West Africa. Also to be mentioned is the work of Claudia W. Moyne, *A List of Films on Africa* (1966), which was meant to meet the specific requirements of Boston University's training program for AID personnel. Foreign films were cited if they could be rented in the United States.

In our own assessment of Africana films, we have drawn on all of the above sources as well as the *Catalogue of French Ethnological Films* (1955), even though these films may be difficult to obtain. We have also used the more complete 408-page *Catalogue Selectif International de Films Ethnographiques sur l'Afrique Noire,* published by UNESCO in 1967. Henry Morgenthau has described this work as follows: "As the first serious attempt at a comprehensive listing and an analytical and critical treatment of the whole body of African ethnographic films, the *Catalogue* is a major landmark." However, none of the films is more recent than 1964. Some of the films listed are available in the United States although they are not so listed. The French films should not be missed just because of the language barrier. Almost every college has a French department which might provide help on translations; or, as suggested earlier, an instructor could turn off the sound track and provide his own narrative.

Several peripheral sources should be mentioned in conclusion. First, the English edition of *Encylopaedia Cinematographica,* published by Pennsylvania State University, has a list of short single-concept films of value to the ethnographer. (These are listed under Social Anthropology.) Second, there is a list of ten films on international affairs in the *Handbook on Africa,* in the Intercome series (Vol. VIII, no. 3, May-June, 1966) published by the Foreign Policy Association. With reference to this work Morgenthau suggests that "the method of selection and the analytical and critical notes represent the kind of approach that would be most useful in compiling comprehensive information on film distribution and general information regarding classroom use of films." Thirdly, there is the *8mm Film Directory* (for 1969–70) by Grace Kone, published by the Educational Film Library Service, which lists short 4- to 10-minute single-concept films.

AUDIOVISUAL AIDS AND *THE AFRICAN EXPERIENCE*

As mentioned earlier, the Program of African Studies at Northwestern University has been exploring the possibilities of developing videotape or EVR cartridges to accompany *The African Experience*. In the meantime, however, it seems useful to list some of the audiovisual aids which can be used as a supplement to the *Syllabus* modules. There has been no attempt to be comprehensive in our coverage of the available materials. Furthermore, we have drawn heavily on existing catalogues and the reputations of particular film producers, rather than systematically previewing all of the materials ourselves. In short, the following list is tentative, illustrative, and of mixed quality. In all cases, however, the item mentioned is regarded as being appropriate to a particular *substantive* topic (or module), and is regarded as having some educational merit. There is no attempt to avoid films on the basis of "political sensitivity," although most of those materials which are derogatory of African life tend to be of poor quality by social-science standards. Some films require the teacher to supplement the narrative, and in many cases to provide the narrative.

We have selected the following list from all of the sources mentioned earlier in this article. An initial selection was made for circulation and comment, and from this list we selected only about 10 per cent of the items for final inclusion.

We have included all types of audiovisual media within each of the module categories, rather than arranging the items by type of media. Some of the materials are more accessible than others (e.g., commercial films) and some are more usable than others (e.g., 35mm films require special equipment). The purpose of inclusion of less accessible items, however, is to stress the fact of their existence. As new technical developments emerge, many of these materials will probably be edited and integrated into more accessible and usable packages.

SELECTED AUDIOVISUAL REFERENCES

The following list of audiovisual references is arranged by module number. The bibliographic format follows that used elsewhere in this volume:
   1. Author/producer's name.
   2. Title of work.
   3. Reference items (including type of medium, length of time, date of production, name of distributor, and rental and/or purchase price).
   4. Annotation and evaluation of the item. All items have been arranged alphabetically within module categories, regarless of type of medium (e.g., 16mm, 8mm, 35mm, filmstrips, records). The addresses of all distributors are listed at the end.

I. African Society and Culture

3. *The African Ethnic Mosaic*

Anon.
The Peoples of Africa
16mm, color, 16 minutes. McGraw-Hill, $180.00.
>Shows the wide range of variation found in the African population: Arabs, Bantu, Pygmies, Masai, Indians, and Europeans. Shows modern Nairobi hospital where Africans of many origins are working together.

Anon.
The Banyoro (Bakitara)
35mm, b&w, silent, 62 minutes. Film Study Center, Harvard University.
>Shows various aspects of ethnic community among the Nyoro of Uganda.

William Bascom
The Yoruba of Nigeria
16mm, color, silent (English subtitles), 50 minutes. Department of Anthropology, Northwestern University.
>Example of one of most developed of African ethnic societies. Views of Ibadan, Meko, Oyo, and Ilesha, and the region of Ekiti in Nigeria. Views of Ibadan and markets, a river trip to Meko where the construction of a house is seen; also a dance on stilts and ifa divination.

CON
The Hunters
16mm, color, sound, 76 minutes, 1958. Rental: Indiana, $25.00; CON, $25.00 b&w, $40.00 color; Penn State, $13.25; NYU, $22.00.
>Example of one of the least developed of African ethnic societies—the Bushmen living in the Kalahari Desert. Follows a hunting party of four Bushmen as they track and kill a giraffe. Identifies the weapons and hunting methods used. Illustrates the village life and portrays the sharing of results of the hunt. Reveals the bare subsistence level of life experienced by the Bushmen.

Simon Ottenburg
The Ibo of Nigeria
16mm, color, silent, 10 minutes, 1952. Department of Anthropology, University of Washington, Seattle.
>Sequences include agriculture, playing of the *okoumkpa*, wrestling, and dances

8. *Family and Kinship*

Jean Rouch

Cimetiere Dans La Falaise (Cemetery in the Cliff)
16mm, color, sound (French), 20 minutes, 1952. Mr. Griaule, 4 Rue de Villersexel, Paris

> During the rainy season in the Dogon country of Mali, a man is drowned in the river. After a priest makes a sacrifice, the body is wrapped in a shroud, and, after further ceremonies, is buried.

Karl J. Tanis
Customs and Life in Africa
16mm, b&w and color, silent, 3 hours, 1948–56. Sudan Interior Mission, 164 W. 74th Street, New York, N.Y.

> Deals with the Fulani of Nigeria: marriage, facial and body scars; also with the Kagora of Nigeria: funeral rites, ironworking, child care, agriculture, etc.

9. Traditional Political Systems

R. E. Bradbury and Francis Speed
(For the Benin Historical Research Scheme, University of Ibadan.)
Benin Kingship Rituals
16mm, color, sound, 30 minutes, 1962. Available through the Medical Illustrations Unit, University of Ibadan, Ibadan, Nigeria, £50.

> Some of the Benin Kingship (Oba) ceremonies performed around the beginning of the new year: (1) a masquerade in honor of the supreme deity; (2) scenes of the Oba making offerings and sacrifices to the spirit of his father, while he receives homage from his chiefs; (3) iron rites commemorating the victory of the reigning dynasty over the hereditary nobles of Benin; (4) the Igwe festival, the highpoint of the year, when Oba's powers are renewed for the coming year.

10. Traditional Economic Systems

William Bascom
Yoruba Crafts
16mm, color, silent (English subtitles), 15 minutes. Department of Anthropology, Northwestern University.

> Spinning and dying of cotton by Yoruba women from Oyo and Meko (Nigeria).

British Information Service
Hausa Village
16mm, b&w, 22 minutes, 1947. CON, $80.00.

> Shows activities in a Hausa village in Northern Nigeria, where all the inhabitants are Muslims. Most of the villagers are farmers who raise two kinds of grain. Others live by net fishing for mudfish. During the hot part of the

day there is weaving, spinning, and netmaking in compounds. The final sequences show preparations for a wedding.

Francis P. Conant
House-building Techniques
16mm, b&w, silent, 5 minutes, 1955. Department of Sociology and Anthropology, University of Massachusetts, Amherst, Mass.

House-construction techniques of the Barawa of Northern Nigeria.

Francis P. Conant
Iron Smithing
16mm, b&w, silent, 5 minutes, 1958. Department of Sociology and Anthropology, University of Massachusetts, Amherst, Mass.

Techniques of iron smithing with the Barawa of Northern Nigeria.

Francis P. Conant
The Manipulation of Plateau Nigerian Agricultural Tools
16mm, b&w, silent, 15 minutes. Department of Sociology and Anthropology, University of Massachusetts, Amherst, Mass.

In the Bauchi region of Nigeria, a Barawa instructor uses a plow to demonstrate techniques of preparing a plot of land and sowing seeds.

Paula Foster
Acholi of Northern Uganda
16mm, b&w and color, silent, 30 minutes, 1955. Paula Foster, 5749 S. Dorchester Avenue, Chicago, Ill. 60637.

Shows briefly several aspects of the domestic life of the Acholi of Uganda, including construction of a house (in color) and sequence of dances (in b&w).

Peter B. Hammond
Yatenga: The Cycle of the Economic Year
16mm, color, silent, 1954–56. Peter B. Hammond, c/o Administrative Science Center, University of Pittsburgh, Pittsburgh, Pa.

Deals with the Mossi kingdom of Yatenga (Upper Volta). Attempts to show the correlation between the annual ceremonies and the economic activities of the Mossi. Each ceremony is related to a particular phase of the economic calendar. This reinforces Mossi perception of the interdependence between the social and supernatural forces of the universe.

M. J. Herskovits
Dahomey
16mm, b&w, silent, 60 minutes, 1931. Deposited at the Department of Anthropology, Northwestern University, Evanston, Ill. Write to Mrs. M. J. Herskovits.

Technology and rituals of the Dahomey people.

Fred Jeannot

Les Grands Cultivateurs du Pays Kabre (The Great Agriculturalists of the Kabre Country)

16mm, b&w, sound, reel one, 15 minutes, reel two, 21 minutes, 1948. Centre National de la Cinematographie, 12 Rue de Lubeck, Paris 16e.

Reel one deals with daily life among the Kabre of Togo. In front of the houses, with their thresholds adorned with cowries, women grind millet in wooden mortars, women potters mold vases, decorate and fire them. It is the season when kapok is sold in the market. A man has just died, and his widow and hired mourners bury him according to the traditional rites, which include dancing and singing funeral songs.

Reel two deals with farming among the Kabre of Togo. Shows men and women working in the fields. The women are planting manioc and the men are building retaining walls in the fields. After sequences showing the clearing of undergrowth, ploughing begins. The opening of the hunt is marked by the Lacou ceremony and the initiation of the young hunters who dance in honor of their elders. The council of headmen meets under the chief, surrounded by his Griots, to discuss the village's affairs.

11. Linguistic Systems

World
Amharic
Records, World, $2.45.

Five 7-inch records, part of the World Foreign Language Series, giving English and Amharic pronunciation of general expressions and vocabulary. 23-page English-Amharic dictionary.

World
Swahili
Records, script. World, $2.45.

Five 7-inch records, part of the World Foreign Language Series, giving English and Swahili pronunciation of general expressions and vocabulary. 24-page English-Swahili dictionary.

WTE
Talking Drums (no. 47)
Tape, 15 minutes. WTE, $2.75.

Discussion of the use and construction of drums, characteristics of "drum language." Drum music used to illustrate narrator's comments.

12. Traditional African Literature

AMIE
The Great Elephant Joke — Big Drum, Little Drum
Record, 1968. AMIE, $4.95.

Two Kikuyu folktales with sound effects. "Big Drum, Little Drum" is a story about a drum family (19 minutes). "The Great Elephant Joke" is a story about an elephant who made friends with a man (19 minutes).

Folkways
Ashanti Folk Tales from Ghana
Record. Folkways, $4.15.
"All Stories are Anansi's," "Anansi, the Oldest of Animals," "Nyame's Well," "Two Feasts for Anansi," "Anansi Plays Dead," and "The Porcupine's Hoe."

13. Conceptual Systems and Religion

Jean Rouch
Les Hommes Qui Font La Pluie (The Rainmakers)
16mm, color, sound, 35 minutes, 1950. Jean Rouch, Musée de l'Homme, Palais de Chaillot, Paris, 16e.
Yenendi ("refreshing") rites of the Songhai tribe in the village of Simiri (Niger). After a seven-month drought, all the inhabitants of the village go to the house of the gods to celebrate the rain festival. To the sound of the violin, played by the chieftain, the people perform the ceremonies which conclude with the sacrifice of a ram. At last the clouds pile up, and the rain pours down. A good scientific documentary for all levels of teaching.

Francis Speed *et al.*
Ifa: Yoruba Divination and Sacrifice
16mm, b&w, sound, 18 minutes. Department of Extra-Mural Studies, University of Ibadan, Ibadan, Nigeria, £ 25.
The film demonstrates the ritual of divination and sacrifice as it was performed on behalf of a patient suffering a chronic psychoneurosis.

Francis and Robin Horton
Duminea, A Festival for the Water Spirits
16mm, color, sound, 20 minutes, 1966. Institute of Education, University of Ibadan, Ibadan, Nigeria, £ 25.
Deals with communal rituals in the village of Soku, in the Eastern Niger Delta (Nigeria). Presents two classes of spirits—the heroes and the water people. The heroes are beings who once lived with men. The water spirits have never lived with men. They are the creators and owners of various rivers and creeks. The heroes are the forces of culture, and the water spirits are the forces of nature.

14. Visual Arts

Francis Speed and Ulli Beier
New Images, Art in a Changing African Society

16mm, color, sound, 25 minutes, 1964. Department of Extra-Mural Studies, University of Ibadan, Ibadan, Nigeria, purchase $112.00; Indiana.

Oshogbo, a town in Western Nigeria, was flourishing center of art and crafts in the nineteenth century. This film shows that modernization changed only the images, media, and function of art, but it still preserves its vitality of traditional times. The film is set against a background of traditional festivals.

15. Music

Brandon
African Musicians
16mm, b&w, sound, 14 minutes, 1957. Penn State, $3.70; Indiana, $4.15.

Pictures and describes a number of common African musical instruments. Indicates the probable origin of the instruments. Among those shown and played are the tom-tom, skin drums, horns of various types, and the xylophone.

Betty Warner Dietz and Michael Olatunji
Musical Instruments of Africa
Book and record, 116 pp., 1965. The John Day Company, 62 W. 45th Street, New York, N.Y. 10036, $5.95.

A description with black-and-white pictures of different types of musical instruments; accompanying record demonstrates sounds of these instruments.

J. Dupont (director)
Danses Congolaises (Congolese Dances)
35mm, b&w, sound (French), 12 minutes, 1947. Société d'Application Cinematographique (S.D.A.C.), 15 Rue Vivienne, Paris, 2e.

Dances filmed during the Ogowe-Congo expedition show the mask dances of the Bateke, Okanda, M'beti, and finally the Ba-Binga Pygmies. Concludes with a sequence of dances which takes place at night, by torchlight. Fine photography, with locally recorded music.

Folkways
Bulu Songs from the Cameroons
Record, script. Folkways, $6.79.

Vocal and instrumental music of the Bulus of the Cameroons. Script gives background material with notes on individual bands.

Folkways
Folk Music of Ethiopia
Record, script. Folkways, $6.79.

Vocal and individual music which samples the diverse music of the various ethnic groups of Ethiopia. Script gives background material and notes on each band.

M. J. Herskovits
West African Films
35mm, b&w, silent, 100 minutes, 1931. Deposited at the Department of Anthropology, Northwestern University, Evanston, Ill. Write to Mrs. M. J. Herskovits.

> Includes dances and religious rituals of the Yoruba and Hausa of Nigeria; dances, agriculture, and technology of Dahomey; and finally the dances and rites of the Ashanti of Ghana.

Barbara W. Merriam and Alan P. Merriam
Bala of Congo
16mm, color, silent, 25 minutes. Barbara W. Merriam, c/o Department of Anthropology, Indiana University.

> Set among the Basongay of Kasai Province, Congo. Musical instruments and techniques of the Bala playing of the drums, xylophones, and kisaaghshi. Also shows making of palm oil and pottery in the village of Lupupa.

Barbara W. Merriam
The Shi, Tutsi, and Ekonda of Congo
16mm, color, 24 minutes, 1951/52. Barbara W. Merriam, c/o Department of Anthropology, Indiana University.

> A voyage through the Congo, sequences on the musical instruments and musical techniques of the country.

Frank Speed and Peggy Harper
Studies in Nigerian Dance No. 1: Tiv Women's Dances
16mm, 10 minutes. Institute of African Studies, University of Ibadan, Ibadan, Nigeria, purchase only, $50.40.

> Good study of traditional Tiv dancing by women.

II. Perspectives on the Past

17. *Continental Origins and Physical Character*

BF
A Look at the Geography of Africa
Filmstrip, 51 frames, color, captioned, script from Africa. BF, Developing Continent Series, No. 1, $6.00.

> 39 photos, 11 maps, and 1 full caption frame. Maps include Africa and various regions in Africa. Major emphasis on physical features: rivers (Nile and Zambezi), mountain and lake regions, rainforest, plains, and Kalahari Desert (30); vegetation and animals (8); ancient Egyptian ruins (5); and types of people (4); summary (3). Captions explain frames. Script supplements captions.

MES
Africa, Physical Features
Filmstrip, 35 frames, color, captioned, script. MES, $10.00.

15 photos, 14 maps, 4 drawings. Combination of maps and photos depicting the major physical features of Africa. An emphasis on geological history and mineral deposits. Captions; statements explaining frames.

18. The Evolution of Man in Africa

AMIE
Africa and the Origin of Man
Record, 12-inch LP, 1967. AMIE $4.95.

Introduction via lecture and occasional question-and-answer to a series of records on African history; lectures explain archaeological evidence relative to early African history, focusing on the writings of ancient scholars, investigations of Leaky, archaeology as a science, activities and accomplishments of "near man" and Stone Age man in East Africa. Teaching ideas listed in brief on enclosure.

EBF
Dr. Leaky and the Dawn of Man
16mm, color, 1967. EBF, 2 versions: 26 minutes, $327.50; 50 minutes, $500.

A National Geographic Society production detailing Leaky's search for the origins of man in Africa; depicts evidence unearthed by Leaky and dramatic reconstruction of skull remains.

20. Early Culture and State Formation

Coronet
Ancient Egypt
16mm, color or b&w, sound, 11 minutes. Indiana, $3.40 color, $2.15 b&w.

Shows scenes of Egyptian landscapes, the Sphinx, and the pyramids. The Nile Valley is located on a map, and its settling 10,000 years ago is described. Lists some of the contributions of Egypt to Western civilization, and pictures some Egyptian art.

EBF
Egypt — Cradle of Civilization
16mm, color or b&w, 12 minutes, 1961. EBF, $60.00 b&w, $120.00 color.
Indiana, $3.90.

Examines the civilization which developed along the Nile River in ancient Egypt. Traces the dependence of the people in the Nile Valley upon the river as a source of water and food. Describes government, art, and architecture of early Egypt. Color is important in this production in showing art.

Hoefler
Ethiopia—Africa's Ancient Kingdom
16mm, color, sound, 1961. Hoefler, $165.00.
  Ethiopian history and heritage.

WSP
Early Art
Filmstrip and record, 65 frames, color, not captioned, recorded narrative, 19 minutes, 1968. WSP.
  61 photos, 4 maps, divided into peoples of East and Central Africa (8), Victoria Falls (1), ancient rock drawings of historical interest (11), West African sculpture (26); recorded narrative describes peoples of East-Central Africa; origins and migration of early man; the ancient kingdoms of Kush, Ethiopia, Zimbabwe, Timbuktu; early art objects and African culture.

21. The Impact of Islam in Africa

Centre Cinematographique Marocain
Moulay-Idriss
35mm, b&w, sound, 11 minutes, 1948. Centre Cinematographique Marocain, 85 Rue Henri Popp, Rabat, Morocco.
  The town is situated in Morocco on the spot where Mulai El-Idriss meditated and was buried. It is an important holy city in Morocco and in the world of Islam. Shows eighth-century ruins, the market, the mosque where the descendant of the Prophet is buried. A city of tents provides shelter for the pilgrims. As an accompaniment to the religious festival there are sideshows, feasts, and fantasias.

DIC
Islam
16mm and super 8mm, 16 minutes. DIC, purchase: 16mm, $180.00; super 8mm, $99.00.
  Relates the influence of Islam on people of the Middle East; the Koran and its use; the concept of the five pillars of Islam: one God, daily prayer, brotherhood, charity, and the pilgrimage. May be useful as an introduction to Islam.

Société B. Derocles
Ramadan
35mm, b&w, sound (French), 20 minutes, 1947. Société des Films "Regent" Jacques Haik, 63 Champs Elysees, Paris 8e.
  Gives a detailed picture of the festivities which go with Ramadan. With the appearance of the new moon, fasting begins. There are men shopping in the markets and caravans coming into camp. With sunset the fast is broken and the night's gaiety begins. Coffee-houses and barbers' shops are full. In

Tunis, a puppet show recalls a local epic; a variety show, with dancing girls and fakir, provides entertainment. Illustrates patterns of the "month of fasting" which are found in Black Africa as well as Mediterranean Africa.

22. *Empires of the Western Sudan*

Atlantis and DIC
Negro Kingdoms of Africa's Golden Age: Ghana, Mali and Songhay
16mm and super 8mm, color, 1968, 17 minutes. Atlantis, $150.00; Indiana.
   The impressive history of three African empires that flourished more than 700 years ago is developed against the background of original African art, artists' re-creations, and on-location photography. Focuses on the climate, geography, history, technology, political structure, and religion of the old empires. Recounts the destructive effect of the slave trade.

28. *Origins and Growth of the Slave Trade*

Jackdaw Paper
The Slave Trade and Its Abolition
Pictures. Jackdaw, $2.95.
   Reproduction of 15 pictures, posters, and primary sources dealing with the slave trade and its abolition.

29. *Abolition and States for Freed Slaves*

Firestone Tire and Rubber Company
Liberia: Africa's Only Republic
16mm, color, 27 minutes. Illinois, $5.00.
   History, geography, and topography of Liberia.

30. *The African Legacy in the Americas*

Folkways
Negro Folk Music of Africa and America
2 records, script. Folkways, $13.58.
   Vol. I: Vocal and instrumental music from the various countries of Africa. Vol. II: Music from Latin America and the United States with emphasis on Haiti and the United States. Provides a wide sampling of Negro music from three continents. Process of selection places emphasis on similarities of music. Script gives an introduction with notes on each band.

Silhouettes
African Origins, 500–1492
Record, 12-inch LP, no script, 19 minutes. Silhouettes, $12.50.

One side of Vol. I of "Silhouettes in Courage" that deals exclusively with the African origins of black American culture: mixes narration with "interview" of known participants from the period 500 to 1492; excellent use of music; focuses on trade, learning, and empires in pre-European Africa; original account of culture and value systems of Africans; useful description of indigenous and tradtional slavery before the Atlantic slave trade.

31. White and Black Migrations in Southern Africa

Thorne
The Boer War
8mm film loops, b&w, script, 4 minutes. Thorne, $12.50.
Depicts several fighting scenes from the Boer War and contemporary re-creation of the events.

33. The Scramble for Africa

Allyn & Bacon
Alpha Map Transparencies: Africa
Transparencies, 1967. Allyn & Bacon, 470 Atlantic Avenue, Boston, Mass. 02210.
Two multicolored, single-sheet transparencies on colonialism and decolonialism. Part of larger set, consisting of 33 maps pertaining to the physical, economic, and cultural characteristics of Africa.

34. African Resistance and Reaction

EFE
Light of Ethiopia
16mm, b&w, sound, 26 minutes. EFE, purchase $150.00.
Scenes of Ethiopia and its ruler, the Emperor Haile Selassie; tells the story of the annexation of Ethiopia by Mussolini's army and the events which followed.

35. The Nature of Colonial Systems

NET, WTTW-TV (Chicago)
Africa: Colonialism
16mm, b&w, sound, 29 minutes. NET, $4.75.
Discusses history, peoples, resources, and economy of Africa as well as the habits and customs of Africa. Considers the strategic position of Nigeria to the United States and the problems of U.S. policy with regard to the rising nationalistic protest against colonialism. Now slightly dated.

36. Study Questions: Perspectives on the Past

Harry A. Gailey, Jr.
The History of Africa in Maps
Book, 1967. Denoyer-Geppert Co., $2.50.

 46 black-and-white maps of Africa and various regions of Africa; sections on geography and major historical events; each map accompanied by explanatory text on facing page.

Hayden Book Company
Africa in Perspective
Transparencies, 1968. Hayden $35.00.

 A set of 18 individual transparencies reproducing the maps in *Africa in Perspective*. Charts included when comparing Africa with selected countries of the world. Physical features (2), tribes (2), history (4), agriculture and mineral products (1), population density (1), African diseases (1), independence (3), income and literacy (2), urbanization (1), African religions (1).

A. M. Healy and E. R. Vere-Hodge
The Map Approach to African History
Book, 3rd ed. UTP, $.65.

 65 black-and-white, clearly drawn maps with detailed explanatory text on the highlights of African history and current problems; includes time-line of African history since 1800.

III. Processes of Social Change

38. Social Change and Modernization in Africa

Atlantis
African Girl . . . Malobi
16mm, color, 11 minutes. Atlantis, purchase $110.00.

 The case study of Ibo people of southern Nigeria, as described through the eyes of a young girl. A recurrent theme is the drive for education at all ages. Food production, community enterprise, markets and trading, social change, and urbanization also are depicted. Teachers' summary is included.

CON
African Village
16mm, color, 17 minutes. CON.

 Case study of small Kissi village in Guinea, emphasizing patterns of social change and continuity.

Fleetwood Films

Land of the Swazis
16mm, 18 minutes. Fleetwood Films, $97.50, purchase only.
  Case study (Swaziland) which shows changes in traditional life brought about
  by technological assistance.

40. *Characteristics of African Personality*

Francis Speed, for Raymond Prince, M.D.
Were ni! He is a Madman
16mm, sound, color, 30 minutes, 1963. Department of Extra-Mural Studies,
University of Ibadan, Ibadan, Nigeria, purchase £ 50.
  An ethnopsychiatric film on the traditional management of psychiatric dis-
  orders by the Yoruba of Nigeria, showing a web of well-developed social
  institutions. The two basic types of institutions include the treatment centers
  managed by herbalists and diviners with specialist knowledge of traditional
  psychiatric therapy; and the cult groups which provide a setting for the
  expression of otherwise socially unacceptable behavior through "possession"
  and "masquerade" dances. The film provides an important insight into
  "social deviation" of personality as defined by Yoruba society.

41. *Personality and Social Change*

British Information Services
Father and Son
16mm, b&w, 12 minutes, 1946. CON.
  Changing ideas in an African village. An old man holds to the old ways while
  his son joins the British Navy and learns new ideas. When the grandson is
  hurt, the young man takes him to the hospital. The old man thinks the witch
  doctor could do better. The child's life is saved by the modern treatment.
  (The film does not give convincing evidence for the value of the son's
  modern education, and is propaganda-oriented.)

McGraw-Hill (Canada)
Family of Ghana
16mm, b&w, sound, 30 minutes. Indiana, $5.40.
  The experiences of a family in Ghana illustrate the culture of that country
  and suggest the striving for new ideas and methods by the younger people.
  The older members of the family cling to tradition. The film dramatizes this
  conflict within a Ghanaian family when the son wishes to acquire a motor-
  ized boat for ocean fishing. Film includes sequences of Accra and of traditional music and dancing.

Leo Rampen (written and narrated by Jean Morrison, Canadian Broadcasting
Corporation)

Identity
16mm, b&w, 24 minutes, 1966. Overseas and Foreign Relations Department, CBC (attention: Mr. Anthony Partridge).

While the commentary is burdened with some preconceived (and perhaps patronizing) notions about African "identity crises," it nevertheless intrudes sparingly on the views of African spokesmen it interviews on the subject. The Nigerian author Chinua Achebe denies that any identity crises are felt by his countrymen or himself.

Marshall Segall (Columbia University Center for Mass Communication)
Gentle Winds of Change
16mm, color, 33 minutes, 1961. Penn State, $11.00; NYU, $12.00; Syracuse University, $8.25.

An examination of individuals from Banyankole ethnic society (Uganda). Part of a study of individual personality differences in the Westernization process. Especially good for sociology and anthropology students.

U.N. International Zone Series
The Healers of Aro
16mm, b&w, 28 minutes. UNOPI, rental $8.00, purchase $130.

Shows community mental-health programs in the Western Region of Nigeria. Stresses the impact of rapid economic and social change on mental disorder.

42. Educational Systems in Africa

British Information Services
Achimota
16mm, sound. NYU, write for rental.

Narrated by Julian S. Huxley, this film describes an educational center consisting, at the time, of a secondary school, a teacher-training institution, and the beginning of university training. Although now dated, the film might still be interesting in showing the development of education in Ghana.

EG
African Children at School
Filmstrip, 40 frames, color, captioned, script, 1962. EG.

All frames show students at school and depict various aspects of mission, public, and Muslim schools. 21 frames show classroom situations. Captions include statements and questions which explain frames.

Canadian Film Institute
East African College
16mm.

Account of student life at Makerere University College in Uganda.

McGraw-Hill
Health and Education: Key to African Development
16mm, color, 1967. CON, write for rental.
   Originally a part of an ABC 4-hour documentary on Africa. Well done.

44. *The New Elites of Africa*

McGraw-Hill
The New Africa: Peoples and Leaders
16mm, color, 15 minutes. McGraw-Hill, rental $12.50, purchase $200.00.
   The film introduces the problem of nation-building in African states and
   explores how some African leaders handle this problem: specifically, how
   much these leaders are willing to accept outside help, and from whom; how
   much foreign influence they allow in their policies; and how much these
   leaders emphasize helping themselves. Originally made for ABC 4-hour
   documentary. Well done.

Methodist Publishing House
New Faces of Africa
16mm, color and b&w, 1959. Methodist Publishing House, rental $12.00 color,
$8.00 b&w.
   Narrated by an African physician, includes comments by leaders such as
   Tom Mboya. Interviews an African pastor, a nurse, a chief, an office worker.
   Emphasis is on Protestant activity in Africa.

45. *The Development of Urban Society*

BIR
Mombasa Port
16mm, color and b&w, sound, 15 minutes. BIR, purchase $125.00 color,
$50.00 b&w.
   Shows Kenya's (and East Africa's) largest port as a conglomeration of modern highways, Arab and Persian mosques, Moorish grillworks, and Portuguese landmarks.

EG
Accra, Ghana
Filmstrip, 45 frames, color, captioned, script, 1962. EG, $6.00.
   43 photos and 2 full captions. General characteristics of the city. Modern
   structures and government buildings (13), markets and traditional sections
   (7), modern industrial influences (4), transportation (6), seaport and facilities
   (6), police force (4), and youth groups (3). Captions: statements explaining
   frames. Full captions: review and summary.

EG
Kenya: Principal Cities
Filmstrip, 43 frames, color, captioned, script, 1962. EG, $6.00.
  40 photos and 3 full captions. Nairobi: functions and buildings (10), Mombasa: history, buildings and their functions (10), port facilities (8), Nakuru: buildings and surrounding countryside (9), Kisumu: housing (native and European) (3). Captions: statements explaining frames. Full captions: review (2) and summary (1).

EG
Leopoldville, Republic of the Congo
Filmstrip, 45 frames, color, captioned, script, 1962. EG, $6.00
  43 photos, one map, and 2 full captions. History (5), Congo River (4), population (1), modern structures (4), transportation (9), education and religion (6), port (1), recreational facilities (10), industries and commerce (3). Captions: statements explaining frames. Full captions: review (2) and summary (1).

EG
Timbuktu, Republic of Mali
Filmstrip, 48 frames, color, captioned, script, 1962. EG, $6.00.
  45 photos, one map, and 2 full captions: history (5), Tuaregs (5), Songhai (2), Muslim religion (4), buildings (8), central market (people and products) (8), foods (9), camel caravans and salt trade (4). Captions: statements explaining frames. Full captions: review and summary.

Illinois, Films of the Nations
Leopoldville
16mm, b&w, sound, 17 minutes. Illinois, rental $3.15.
  Shows Leopoldville (now Kinshasa), capital of the former Belgian Congo, as a city of modernity and high standards of living. Industries and customs of daily life are shown. Slightly dated.

46. The Nature of Urban Life

Edinburgh/BBC-TV (Scotland; Marfield.)
Boom Town, West Africa
16mm, b&w, sound, 26 minutes. Indiana, $6.40.
  Depicts the life of the Kamara family of Sierra Leone and shows how their life has been affected by industrialization. Indicates the growth of the village in which they live and the cultural changes through which the people are passing. Discusses the dissolution of tribal customs and formation of young people's organizations which tend to replace tribal organization.

Jean Rouch and Jacques Godbout (National Film Board of the Ivory Coast)
Ceux Qui Parlent Francais: Rose et Landry (Those Who Speak French: Rose and Landry)
16mm, b&w, 28 minutes, 1963. National Film Board of the Ivory Coast, Abidjan.

> Henry Morgenthau writes: "A *cinema verité* dramatic documentary, it is a good example of Rouch's non-ethnographic work. It was filmed mostly in the new business and residential districts of Abidjan, where we find a boy confronted by the problems of modern city life. . . . Landry makes it all quite clear when he says, 'We are destined to forget our past, but I don't think it's good.' "

SVE
How People Live in Kano (Nigeria) and Nairobi (Kenya)
Filmstrip, 53 frames, color, noncaptioned, script, record, 13 minutes. SVE, $9.50.

> 45 photos, 3 maps, drawings, and 3 full captions. Filmed with narration by students in Kano and Nairobi. Introduction; Kano—general characteristics of the land and people; Nairobi—emphasis on modern buildings, schools, churches. History of both cities included. Script follows record. Also available without record.

47. Problems of Urbanization

ICF
City Life in West Africa
8mm film loop, color, 4 minutes, script, 1967. ICF, regular 8mm $16.00, super 8mm $19.50.

> Overview of an African city, showing its various functions and types of structures. Contrasts old and new parts of city, depicts streets scenes, markets and new constructions. Examines impact of Europeans.

Ousman Sembene (Grove Press Film Division)
Mandabi
16mm, 90 minutes. Grove Press.

> The first film about urban life in contemporary Africa made by African filmmakers. Depicts how a remnant of traditional society is overwhelmed by the pace of changing times. Very well received at 1969 New York Film Festival.

48. Spatial Aspects of Transportation and Communications

DIC
Transportation in West Africa
8mm film loop, 4 minutes, 1968. DIC, super 8mm $19.50, regular 8mm $16.00.

Methods of moving people and materials are shown: carrying loads on the head, pushing hand carts, donkeys, camels, canoes, cars, trucks, ships, and airplanes.

EG

Nigeria: Land, Transportation, Communication
Filmstrip, 46 frames, color, captioned, script, 1964. EG, $6.00.

42 photos, one map, and 3 full captions; major emphasis on physical geography: terrain, vegetation, and climate (20), transportation (11), postal and radio communication (7), palm oil (4). Captions: statements explaining frames. Full captions: review (2) and summary questions (1).

EG

Republic of Senegal: Transportation and Cities
Filmstrip, 46 frames, color, captioned, script, 1962. EG, $6.00.

43 photos and 3 full captions. Major emphasis on the city of Dakar: history (2), transportation and communication (14), modern buildings, markets, recreation, and historical buildings (27). Captions: statements explaining frames. Full captions: review (2) and summary questions (1).

50. The Impact of Christianity

AF

Conquest of Darkness
16mm, color, sound, 28 minutes. AF, rental free.

How the Salvation Army aids the blind in Africa.

Anon. (produced for the White Fathers)
Doctor Coarisson
16mm, color, sound. AF, rental $4.00.

Story of a priest with several medical degrees who is working as a medical missionary at Ouagadougou (Upper Volta).

Anon. (produced for the White Fathers)
The Catechist
16mm, color, sound, 20 minutes. AF, rental $4.00.

Story of the conversion of Joanne Kitegana, one of the first of the African lay missionaries and teachers.

Anon. (produced for the White Fathers)
The White Fathers
16mm, color, sound, 15 minutes. AF, rental $4.00.

Testimonial by Arch Oboler to the work of the White Fathers of Africa, a Roman Catholic missionary society.

CAFM

Africa and Schweitzer
16mm, b&w, sound, 28 minutes. CAFM, rental $10.00.
Review of Schweitzer's life, his founding of the mission in Gabon, and his medical service. Narrated by Lowell Thomas.

CON
Albert Schweitzer
16mm, color and b&w, sound, 80 minutes, 1958. CON: color, rental $60.00, purchase $500; b&w, rental $45.00, purchase $350.00.
Biography of Schweitzer, who wrote the narrative, tracing his life from birth through the time of his decision at the age of 30 to start his rainforest hospital. Records a typical day at Lambarene (Gabon).

DKB
The Mission
16mm, color, sound, 33 minutes, 1962. DKB, purchase $300.00.
Activities of OLA missionaries throughout the former Federation of Nigeria in schools, training colleges, hospitals, maternity wards, a leper colony, and an operation theater. Visit of Pope Paul VI, as former Cardinal Montini of Milan, while on tour of West Africa.

FMGM
African Harvest
16mm, b&w, sound, 43 minutes, 1950. FMGM, write for rental.
African missions operated by the General Mission Board of the Free Methodist Church. Describes various installations and the educational and medical as well as the evangelistic programs.

Methodist Publishing House
Congo Journey
16mm, b&w, sound, 30 minutes, 1958. Methodist Publishing House, rental $6.00.
Tour of Methodist missions in the Belgian Congo shows variety of rural and urban ministries at Lidja, Katako, Kombe, and Leopoldville.

National Council of Churches
Africa Disturbed
16mm, color, 28 minutes, 1960. National Council of Churches, purchase $150.00.
An interview with Dr. Emory Ross, a missionary who spent 21 years in the Congo and who traveled through the new nations of Africa. Suggests by illustration of several countries the "disturbing" influence of education, technical achievements, and money economy. Various leaders, including Tom Mboya, discuss conditions, influence of Christianity, pro- and anti-American feeling. Emphasis is on Christian impact.

IV. Consolidation of Nation-States

55. *Patterns of African Nationalism*

African Productions, Ltd.
Mau Mau
16mm, b&w, 20 minutes, 1955. CON, apply for rental.

> A brief resume of the Mau Mau movement in Kenya. Opens with terrorist violence of the movement and outlines administration efforts to combat the Mau Mau. Emphasis is placed on record of economic and social development by the administration. Attacks Mau Mau movement as agitation by native malcontents. Yet authentic newsreel shots make it a useful historical document, despite its biased and short-sighted approach.

CON. Edward R. Murrow report.
Report from Africa, Part I
16mm, 28 minutes, 1956. Indiana, $4.90.

> Edward R. Murrow reports on events in Kenya, Ghana, and Liberia. Emphasis in Kenya is on the Mau Mau movement.

NET
Twentieth Century Revolutions in World Affairs: The Revolution in the Colonial World
16mm, b&w, sound, 29 minutes. Indiana, $5.40.

> Discusses the revolution that has taken place in the colonial world and the present conflict between the remaining colonial powers of the West and the newly independent countries of Asia and Africa. Points out the major issues by condensed re-enactment of the U.N. committee debate on Algeria in 1955. Shows the reaction of the French delegation when the question of Algeria was voted upon. Concludes by pointing out the problems and methods of coping with colonialism.

NET
Algeria—What Price Freedom?
16mm, 54 minutes. Indiana, $8.15.

> Presents Algeria struggling to establish a stable government and a higher standard of living. Uses inserts of the seven-year war for independence. Visits one family which is quite Europeanized and yet traditional in many ways. Indicates the slowness of the change in status and behavior of women. Provides a brief account of the school system in transition and the challenge of illiteracy.

56. *Independence*

CON, National Film Board of Canada

Road to Independence
16mm, 29 minutes, 1957. CON, $8.00.
> Political developments in 1957 in Ghana, Nigeria, Nyasaland (now Malawi), and the other former colonial territories.

Embassy of Congo (Kinshasa)
Festivities Commemorating Independence
16mm, 15 minutes. Embassy of Congo (Kinshasa), free rental.
> Shows independence activities in cities such as Kinshasa, Kisangani, Matadi, Mbujimaji, and Lubumbashi, including the parades of Congolese troops, students, and workers.

Ghana government
Free Forever
16mm, b&w, sound, 30 minutes. Ghana.
> Record of Ghana's first independence anniversary celebration in March, 1958.

National Film Board of Canada
The Hour of Independence
16mm, 28 minutes. CON, $8.00.
> Taking the example of Algeria, the film tries to explore the question of "what now, after independence." The film turns to respected voices of independence in former French colonies. Distinction made between the "pragmatical" course of English colonial rulers and the more "mystical" mission of the French.

U.N.
A New Future for Somaliland
16mm, b&w, 10 minutes. UNOPI, $1.25.
> After the war, the United Nations decided to apply the International Trusteeship System to Somaliland, which enabled territories and peoples to prepare for either self-government or independence. Film shows the Italian Trusteeship Administration carrying out the program and how young Somali students study modern developments.

UNOPI
End of a Chapter
16mm, 1962. UNOPI.
> As most of its "wards" achieve independence or self-government, the United Nations Trusteeship System nears the end of its history. The progress of twenty million people in eleven territories of Africa and the Pacific has been guided by this unique international link between the governing and the governed. Shows life in present and former U.N. Trust Territories, including New Guinea, Somalia, Togoland, and Tanganyika.

57. Interethnic Integration

McGraw-Hill
Kenya: The Multi-Racial Experiment
16mm, color, 1967. CON, write for rental.
> Originally part of the ABC 4-hour documentary on Africa shown in 1967. Well done.

NET
Africa: The Hidden Frontiers
16mm, b&w, sound, 59 minutes (2 reels), 1963–64. Indiana, $8.15.
> Documents Kenya's attempts to unify its numerous ethnic groups and its European and Asian peoples into a coherent nation. Explores the contrasting ways of life of several dominant groups, plus the influence of European and Asian settlers. Contrasts rural life with a visit to the melting pot of Nairobi and shows Kenyatta speaking to a gathering.

59. Territorial Integration and Boundaries

UCOL, Hearst Movietown News
Powder Keg in the Congo
16mm, b&w, sound, 11 minutes. UCOL, $2.25.
> Describes the Congo and traces its development under Belgian rule: cities rose but there was no education program or political development. Portrays the activities of Lumumba, Kasavubu, the Congolese Army, and Tshombe; the entry of U.N. forces in the Congo; Russia's attack on United Nations' meeting.

UNOPI
Question in Togoland
16mm, color, 20 minutes, 1957. UNOPI, rental $8.50, purchase $180.00.
> A pictorial report showing how a U.N.–supervised plebiscite brought former British Togoland into the newly formed state of Ghana.

60. The Role of Ideology in Nation-Building

Henry Morgenthau III (WGBH-TV, Boston, for NET)
Tanzania: The Quiet Revolution
16mm, 60 minutes, 1965. Indiana, $9.15.
> A portrait of the geography and peoples of Tanzania and their struggle with the problems of poverty, illiteracy, and races. Interviews with President Nyerere. Excellent film for college level.

61. Types of Civilian Regimes

Ghana government
Republic
16mm, color, sound, 50 minutes. Ghana, free.

> Inauguration of Dr. Nkrumah as President, and Ghana Republic celebrations in July, 1960.

63. Participation and Mobilization

VEC
Eritrea — The African Votes
Filmstrip, 22 frames, b&w, captioned, script. VEC, $4.00.

> 17 photos, 2 maps, and 3 full captions. Preparation and election of a new representative assembly by the people. Maps and captions deal with history (4). Captions: statements explaining frames. Full captions on vocabulary.

64. Elite Instability and Military Rule

McGraw-Hill
Ghana
16mm, color, 14 minutes. CON, write for cost.

> "Most up-to-date film presently available on Ghana. Originally part of the ABC 4-hour documentary on Africa shown in 1967. Very well done." Made after the military coup against Nkrumah.

Moral Re-Armament
You Can Count on Us
16mm, b&w, sound, 14 minutes. AF, $5.00.

> Military and ideological training of the Congolese Army, filmed in Leopoldville (now Kinshasa) and on maneuvers in the interior with the 1st Para-Commando Battalion.

65. The Implications of Nigeria-Biafra

ABC News
The Problem of Nigerian Unity
16mm, color, 19 minutes, 1967. McGraw-Hill; Indiana, $8.15.

> The purpose of the film is to introduce the concept of "tribalism" and show how competition and animosity have undermined attempts to create a unified Nigeria. Shows the conflicts between Muslim and Christian influences. Originally part of ABC 4-hour documentary. Well done.

Atlantis
Africa Awakens: Modern Nigeria
16mm, color, sound, 23 minutes, revised in 1966. Indiana, $6.65.

> Depicts various peoples of Nigeria and their accomplishments and reviews

African history from the Islamic spread in the seventh century. Statuary is pictured from the slavery period. The civilian government with its constitiutional proceedings and elections is seen as an outgrowth of British influence. Discusses the Hausa, Yoruba, and Ibo ethnic groups. Concludes with comments on modernization in Africa. Now dated.

Atlantis
Nigeria: Problems of Nation-Building
16mm, color, 22 minutes, 1967. Atlantis, purchase $200.00.

Geography, pre-colonial and colonial history, religion, language, and economic development are analyzed in this realistic appraisal of the problems of national unity. Emphasis is placed on ethnic hostilities and conflict between traditional and innovative segments of society. Helps to explain Biafran secession. Teachers' summary.

Paul Bohannan
Africa in Change: West Africa (Nigeria)
16mm, color and b&w, 1962. Boston University, $10.00 color, $5.20 b&w; Indiana, $7.65 color, $4.65 b&w.

Moyne of BU writes: "A good general introduction to Nigeria. Pictures the cultural, religious and economic differences of the regions. Emphasizes the role of education in uniting varied peoples."

McGraw-Hill (Canada)
Nigeria: Giant in Africa
16mm, b&w, sound, 52 minutes (2 reels). Indiana, $9.40.

Recounts the history of Nigeria to 1960. Begins with a description of the three regions and cultures of the major ethnic groups. Tells how this nation of "40 million" united to elect their representatives who were to structure their territories into a united, independent, and modern nation. Shows the traditional life that exists beside the modern changes that have been adopted under the leadership of the first Federal Prime Minister, Abubakar Balewa. Now dated in terms of perspective.

NET
Children in the Balance: The Tragedy of Biafra
16mm, b&w, 60 minutes. Indiana, rental $13.00, purchase $240.00.

Depicts the starvation, death, and disease of children caught in the civil war between Nigeria and Biafra.

Shell B.P.
Nigeria: Framework for a Nation
16mm, color, 1963. Nigerian Embassy, free.

Film shows the juxtaposition of old and new in Nigeria. Narrated by Yinka Olumide. Discusses Nigeria's economic problems and what the country is doing about them. A good picture of the nation's resources and its needs. Political and social aspects are omitted. Although dated, still very useful.

69. An Assessment of Resources

CG

The Copper Belt of Central Africa

Filmstrip, 27 frames, color, noncaptioned, script, 1959. CG, $8.50.

> 26 photos and one map. Terrain and vegetation (2), mining activities (10), types of housing and settlements (8), social services (4), transportation (2). Script provides title and paragraph on each frame.

70. Agricultural Reorganization

Association Films, Inc. (Firestone Tire and Rubber Co.)

A Changing Liberia

16mm, color, mid-1950s. Association Films, Broad at Elm Streets, Ridgefield, N. J. 07657, free rental.

> A survey of Liberia against the background of the production of rubber. Narration and scenes skip around and the film is not very well organized. The emphasis is on rubber and the work of Firestone.

DIC

Rubber Plantation in West Africa

8mm film loops, 4 minutes, 1968. DIC, super 8mm $19.50, regular 8mm $16.00.

> On the plantation and in the processing plant the production of raw rubber is viewed step by step from latex tapping to the shipment of bulk elastic blocks overseas. Filmed in Liberia, the sequence introduces the climatic conditions favorable to production of this important material.

DIC

Peanuts—Important Produce of West Africa

8mm film loops, 4 minutes, 1968. DIC, super 8mm $19.50, regular 8mm $16.00.

> Shows peanut ("groundnut") production from harvesting to exportation· women harvesting, shelling by hand-operated machines, bagging and hauling by donkeys to storage mounds for export. Filmed in northern Nigeria, this sequence is useful for introducing the products and climate of the inland savanna as opposed to the coastal rainforest of West Africa.

DIC

Agriculture in West Africa

8mm film loops, silent, 1968. DIC, super 8mm $19.50, regular 8mm $16.00.

> The harvesting of crops and livestock herding are shown in both wet and dry areas of West Africa. Air shots of farms are seen, as well as patterns of irrigation. This film may be used to illustrate both the products and the problems of farming in West Africa.

UU
Ethiopia Advances
16mm, sound, 10 minutes. UU, $1.25.

Efforts of the United Nations Food and Agriculture Organization in Ethiopia. Shows that the extremely fertile soil of the country can often produce three crops a year. Shows work of U.N. experts with local chiefs and district governors, and FAO activities in vaccination of cattle.

71. The Industrialization Process

EG
Republic of the Ivory Coast: Industries, Products and Cities
Filmstrip, 46 frames, color, captioned, script, 1962. EG, $6.00.

44 photos and full captions. Emphasis divided between agriculture and urban centers. Agriculture and agricultural products (14), Abidjan (buildings, industries and products) (20), Bouake (surrounding regions, markets and products) (10). Captions: statements explaining frames. Full captions: review (1) and summary questions (1).

Ghana government
Industrial Development in Ghana
16mm, b&w, sound, 30 minutes. Ghana.

Examines the industrial situation in Ghana and recounts the various facilities in the country for foreign investors.

ICF
Labor in West Africa
8mm film loops, color, 4 minutes, 1967. ICF, super 8mm $16.00; DIC, super 8mm $19.50, regular 8mm $16.00.

Men, women, and children are seen at various types of skilled and unskilled labor. Workers are shown constructing bridges and houses, surveying roads, and packing nuts. This film is useful in illustrating the variety of labor skills in West Africa.

73. Development of Economic Systems

DIC
Markets in West Africa
8mm film loops, 4 minutes, 1968. DIC, super 8mm $19.50, regular 8mm $16.00.

Market scenes of all types, from downtown department stores to calabash gourd vendors, are seen in this panorama of West African goods and sales techniques. An introduction to the many types of goods available in West Africa and to their influence upon the standard of living.

McGraw-Hill
The Economy of Africa
16mm, color or b&w, 13 minutes, 1966. McGraw-Hill and Florida State University, rental $6.10, purchase $180.00.

> Offers glimpses of the efforts made by independent governments to change from subsistence farming to a cash crop economy. Depicts how problems of infertile soil, rainforest, and barter economy have succumbed to road building, government-built suburbs, and technical training schools. Explains the main difficulty in attempting to develop industries as being due to reluctance of foreign manufacturers to invest capital.

McGraw-Hill Filmtext (Minerva Films Ltd.)
Tanzania: Progress Through Self-Reliance
16mm, color, 20 minutes. McGraw-Hill, rental $12.50, purchase $260.00.

> A study of African socialism responding to the challenge of development. Emphasizes the potential strength of people working together. The film highlights the Kilimanjaro district, the Southern Highlands, and the regions south of Lake Victoria, which are centers of agricultural and industrial innovation. Viewers will see a cooperative society at work and gain an insight into the economic problems of developing African nations.

75. Technology and Nation-Building

ACI (for McGraw-Hill)
Northern Africa: Water and Man
16mm, color, sound, 17 minutes. Indiana, $6.40.

> Describes basic geographic features of this dry and barren region. Shows how the Nile water-power is being controlled through dam and irrigation projects for agricultural and hydroelectric purposes. Discusses the agricultural and industrial development relating the area's dependence on its coastal cities for continued economic growth, and reports the implications of the discovery of oil.

British Information Service, CON
They Planted a Stone
16mm, b&w, sound, 27 minutes. CON, rental $7.00, purchase $110.00.

> How the desert of the Sudan was tranformed, by harnessing the waters of the Nile, into the rich country of the Cezira Cotton Scheme. Contrasts the life of a Sudanese man in the village of Remeitab, with the possibilities for his children in the future.

Ghana government
Skilled Workers
16mm, b&w, sound, 18 minutes. Ghana.

> Produced to encourage technical education in Ghana, serves as an appeal to

young Ghanaians to prepare themselves for skilled jobs during the National Technical and Apprenticeship Week, September 14–21, 1961.

V. Africa and the Modern World

78. Emergent Patterns of Regionalism

Newsweek
The East Africa Common Market
Chart, single sheet 30 × 45 inches, January, 1968. Newsweek.
   Consists of two maps: large map of the continent of Africa with all countries, nations comprising the East Africa Common Market identified; smaller map showing just the countries in the Common Market and their major products. Notes on the development of economic cooperation and the formation of the Common Market. Accompanying spirit master with map of Africa and map research and discussion question.

79. Pan-Africanism and Continental Unity

Ghana government
Freedom for Africa
16mm, b&w, sound, 30 minutes, 1958. Ghana, free.
   Record of the conference of Independent African States held in Accra in April, 1958.

81. Africa at the United Nations

CON, released by the U.N.
The Trusteeship Council and System
16mm, b&w, sound, 15 minutes. CON, rental $5.00, purchase $75.00.
   How non-self-governing peoples are helped toward effective administration of their own choosing by the U.N., using Somaliland as an example.

U.N. and CON
Man in the Blue Helmet
16mm, 28 minutes. CON, $7.50; Penn State, $4.75.
   U.N. work in the Congo and Gaza strip in 1960. Narrated by Alistair Cooke.

82. Africa and the Former Metropoles

CAFM
Africa: The French Community
Filmstrip, 41 frames, b&w, captioned. CAFM, $6.00.

28 photos, 6 maps, 2 drawings, and 5 full captions. Deals with French colonialism and the evolution of the French community. Depicts French relationships with African states in French Community in area of trade, aid, and organization. Captions: statements explaining and supplementing frames.

Indiana, Research Collection
The Economics of Empire
16mm, b&w, sound, 29 minutes. In research collection, Indiana.

Discusses the economics of imperialism from pure exploitation to the modern concept of aid and development. Explains Lenin's thesis of imperialism, its present-day validity, and the appeal of this doctrine to the countries of Africa, Asia, and the Middle East. Analyzes various forms of economic imperialism.

NET
The Volunteers
16mm, b&w, sound, 55 minutes (2 reels). Indiana, $8.90.

Reviews work of young British volunteers (Volunteers for Services Overseas) in the African country of Malawi. Shows volunteers at work in the villages. Presents the volunteers' reasons for coming to Malawi, their frustrations and successes, and evaluates their work.

UWF
Republic of the Ivory Coast (The Peoples of Africa Series)
16mm, b&w, 20 minutes, 1967. UWF.

Depicts export-oriented economy and products of the Ivory Coast. Emphasis on growth and potential economic ties with France. (Also included are scenes of an Independence Day celebration in a small town, illustrating a blending of modern and traditional life in the Ivory Coast.) Gives indication of the close linkages which have persisted in the independence era between France and Ivory Coast.

83. Africa and the United States

McGraw-Hill
Crossroads Africa: Pilot for a Peace Corps
16mm, b&w, 54 minutes, 1961. McGraw-Hill, $250.00.

Documents the work of fifteen American college and graduate students helping the villagers in Guinea build a reception center in 1960. Introduced by President Kennedy, with additional comments by R. Sargent Shriver, then head of the Peace Corps, and narrated by Edward R. Murrow.

NF
The New Africa

16mm, b&w, sound, 35 minutes. NF, purchase $73.00.

As Assistant Secretary of State for African Affairs, Joseph C. Satterthwaite discusses basic problems facing emerging African nations.

87. *The Remnants of Colonialism*

EG

Lourenço Marques: Mozambique

Filmstrip, 45 frames, color, captioned, script, 1964. EG, $6.00.

41 photos, one map, and 3 full captions. City's functions (3), modern structures (11), recreation (11), education (4), industries and products (12). Captions: statements explaining frames. Full captions: review (2) and summary (1).

EG

South-West Africa (Continent of Africa; South Africa Series.)

Filmstrip, 42 frames, color, captioned, script, 1962. EG, $6.00.

38 photos, one map, and 3 full captions. General overview of region. Climate and terrain (6), resources (9), people (12), cities and ports (8), transportation (3). Captions: statements explaining frames. Full captions: review (2) and summary (1).

EG

Angola: Important Cities

Filmstrip, 46 frames, color, captioned, script, 1962. EG, $6.00.

43 photos and 3 full captions. Cities: Luanda (24), Benguela and Mocamedes (8), and Nova Lisboa (2); buildings, economic activities and transportation, people of cities (9). Captions: statements explaining frames. Full captions: review (2) and summary (1).

EG

Luanda: Angola

Filmstrip, 46 frames, color, captioned, script, 1954. EG, $6.00.

42 photos, one map, and 3 full captions. History (5), housing (9), role of Catholic Church (4), recreation (10), industries and commerce (14). Captions: statements explaining frames. Full captions: review (2) and summary (1).

NBC

Angola: Journey to a War

16mm, b&w, sound, 54 minutes. CON, rental $15.00, purchase $250.00.

Attempts to show both sides of the bitter conflict between Portugal and Angola which broke out in March, 1961. Shows nationalist rebels training, displaced people routed from their homes by Portuguese bombs, missionary work at the hospital at Kupese. Narrated by Chet Huntley.

UNOPI

Decolonisation in Africa

16mm, b&w, 18½ minutes, 1967. UNOPI.

The U.N. Special Committee of 24 on the ending of colonialism traveled to Africa in 1967 to visit southern African nationalist leaders in exile in the cities of Kinshasa, Kitwe, and Dar es Salaam. A U.N. film team covered the meetings held with various leaders and interested parties dealing with the problems of decolonization. This film gives an unusual glimpse of a U.N. committee at work in the field. Excellent film for use at college level. Includes interviews with African leaders from Angola, Mozambique, Southern Rhodesia, and South-West Africa. Film is also available through McGraw-Hill, entitled "A Mission to Africa."

UNOPI

United Nations Seminar on Apartheid, Racial Discrimination and Colonialism in Southern Africa

16mm, b&w, 15 minutes. UNOPI, rental $6.00, purchase $75.00.

This international seminar was held in Kitwe, Zambia, under the U.N. auspices to provide a forum for speakers who might not otherwise have a chance to make their views known. A U.N. film crew records the sights and sounds of a part of Africa's emerging political consciousness as expressed by participants of the seminar. Frank criticisms of certain conditions are expressed.

88. Race Relations in Southern Africa

BBC-TV

White Africa—Apartheid

16mm, b&w, 40 minutes. Robeck, rental $30.00, purchase $300.00.

An attempt to understand the mind of the white South African, while not condoning his point of view. According to the film, the white South African considers the black man different and inferior. Outnumbered 4 to 1, the white South African feels that his way of life is threatened by the modernization of the black majority. The film questions the South African claim that whites know what is best for the black majority.

EG

Johannesburg: Republic of South Africa

Filmstrip, 42 frames, color, captioned, script, 1962. EG, $6.00.

42 photos and 3 full captions. Major emphasis on industry and commerce of city: location and surrounding region (4), commerce and industry (15), population (housing, occupations, ethnic groups) (10), transportation (3), education and cultural activities (7), buildings (4). Captions: statements explaining frames. Full captions: review (2) and summary (1).

Kent Mackenzie, Lionel Rogosin, and Carl Lerner
Come Back Africa
16mm, b&w, sound, 84 minutes. CON, rental $75.00-$100.00.

Made in secret (the South African police were told a musical travelogue was being made) with a nonprofessional cast. General message is one of despair, the South African atmosphere being charged with the extreme forms of racial tension. Excellent film for college level.

National Film Board of Canada (McGraw-Hill)
Black and White in South Africa
16mm, b&w, sound, 30 minutes. Indiana, $4.90.

Reports on developments within South Africa regarding apartheid. Recounts historical events, including arrival of the Dutch (Boers), the British settlers, the Great Trek, and the Boers' battle with the Zulus; the Boer War; the political victory of the Afrikaner Nationalists. Indicates the beliefs which underlie the conflicts between the Bantu, the British, and the Boers. Outlines the present South African government policy and projects future conflicts.

NET
South African Essay: Fruit of Fear
16mm, b&w, 60 minutes. Indiana, rental $9.15, purchase $200.00.

Documents and contrasts the two societies existing in South Africa today—the black majority and the ruling white minority. Interviews leaders of both groups regarding their views of apartheid. Film contrasts social and economic opportunities of the two groups.

89. Politics and Race in South Africa

NET
South African Essay Part II: One Nation, Two Nationalisms
16mm, b&w, 60 minutes. Indiana, $9.15.

Uses documentary film footage to examine the South African National Party (white) and the policy of strict separation of people according to racial origins. Features interviews with leaders from the several racial groups involved. Examines the political machinery which enforces apartheid.

WTTW-TV (Chicago)
Africa: South Africa (America Looks Abroad)
16mm, b&w, 29 minutes. In research collection, Indiana.

Discusses the South African government's policy of rigid segregation and speculates on the future effects. Presents the views of a white and a black South African on the apartheid policy.

90. Contemporary African Literature

CBC (Leo Rampen)
Identity
16mm, color, 27 minutes. Write CBC for rental.

Prominent African writers (e.g., Chinua Achebe of Nigeria and Bernard Fonlon of Cameroon) discuss African dilemmas and attitudes toward questions of identity.

NET
African Writers of Today, Program 1: Walter Allen, Amos Tutuola, Ulli Beier
16mm, b&w, sound, 30 minutes. Indiana, $4.90.

Introduces series host Lewis Nkosi, who begins survey of Africa's writers with English evaluation by critic Walter Allen. Film shifts to Nigeria with Amos Tutuola, author of *The Palm Wine Drinkard,* etc., who talks of the past and Yoruba story-telling ways. Ends with Ulli Beier, German-born former editor of African literary magazine *Black Orpheus* (published in Nigeria).

NET
African Writers of Today, Program 2: David Rubadiri, Léopold Sédar Senghor, Bernard Fonlon, Wole Soyinka
16mm, b&w, sound, 30 minutes, 1964. Indiana, $4.90.

Examines French African literature and the concept of negritude, the idea of a unique African collective personality. Visits a classroom in Malawi where the teacher-poet Rubadiri discusses Soyinka's poem "Telephone Conversation." Presents President Senghor of Senegal, also an admired poet, who speaks on negritude. Closes with Dr. Fonlon in Cameroon, who discusses dangers facing African literature.

NET
African Writers of Today, Program 3: Ezekiel Mphahlele
16mm, b&w, sound, 30 minutes, 1964. Indiana, $4.90.

Presents an interview with exiled South African essayist and short story writer, Mphahlele, who discusses the advantages and disadvantages of a writer in exile. Reveals that he feels he has absorbed both the European and African traditional life but remains gloomy about creative writing in a divided society. Discusses the author's autobiography.

NET
African Writers of Today, Program 4: Chinua Achebe
16mm, b&w, sound, 30 minutes, 1964. Indiana, $4.90.

Opens with an interview involving Nkosi, Soyinka, and featured guest, Achebe. Focuses on the craft and work of Achebe himself and questions whether he deliberately avoids passing moral judgment. Shows Achebe discussing the influences which have shaped his artistic life and recounting experiences from a recent U.S. visit. Closes with an examination of the traditional novel and the possibility of a new African novel form.

NET
African Writers of Today, Program 6: David Rubadiri
16mm, b&w, sound, 30 minutes, 1964. Indiana, $4.90.

Mr. Nkosi interviewing poet and educator David Rubadiri of Malawi and Kenyan poet Joseph Kariuki. Discusses Rubadiri's personal struggle as a creative writer in an emerging nation and the general state of contemporary African literature. Describes influence of oral tradition in African writing; discusses possible future forms, and examines how African literature is taught in the schools.

91. Contemporary Social Thought

NET
African Writers of Today, Program 5: William Abraham
16mm, b&w, sound, 30 minutes. Indiana, $4.90.

Presents Nkosi and Soyinka in Accra interviewing Professor Abraham, philosopher and author of *The Mind of Africa*. Focuses in detail on the function of the writer in Africa.

NET
Léopold Sédar Senghor
16mm, b&w, sound. Indiana, $5.40.

Introduces Léopold Sédar Senghor, his poetry, and the environment which his poems reflect. Discusses his philosophy concerning the blending of the African and the Western cultural traditions. Describes Senghor as the poet laureate and president of the Republic of Senegal and presents, in English, readings of five of his poems.

Jonathan Wise Polier
Africa Speaks
16mm, b&w, sound, 18 minutes, 1961. Brandon, rental $5.00, purchase $90.00; Indiana, $4.15.

Problems of contemporary Africa discussed by five African university students in Paris. They discuss neutralism, nationalism, and political development. An American student joins in their discussion on the matter of the Negro in America. English narration over the actual conversations in French. Now slightly dated, but good for college level.

92. Urban Design and Architecture

DIC

Homes in Africa

8mm film loop, 4 minutes, 1960. DIC, super 8mm $19.50, regular 8mm $16.00.
Many examples of urban and rural homes throughout different climatic
regions of Africa are seen in this film. Aerial photography shows different
parts of the continent where strong Islamic and European influences are
seen as well as purely indigenous styles.

Ghana government

Tema Harbor City

16mm, b&w, sound, 40 minutes. Ghana, free.
The story of Tema (Ghana) is seen through the eyes of a family of local
inhabitants. The tiny fishing village springs up into a modern city with trade,
industry, and social activity, and serves as the port for the capital city of
Accra.

93. Visual Arts and Music

Folkways

Dahomey Suite for Oboe and Piano

Record, script. Folkways, $5.79.
Side 1: The Dahomey Suite. Blending of the non-harmonic structures of
West African songs with the harmonic-polyphonic language of the contemporary music. Side 2: samples of African music to provide a comparison with
the "Afro-European" idiom of the Suite. Both vocal and instrumental music.
Samples not confined to West Africa. Script: introduction with notes on each
band.

Folkways

Psalms of the Cameroons

Records, script. Folkways, $5.79.
Collection of psalms sung by the people of Cameroon. Script provides
English translations of the psalms.

Les Troubadours du Roi Baudouin

Missa Luba

Record, script. Philips, $4.90.
Combination of traditional Congolese songs and Christian liturgy. A mass is
sung in Congolese fashion, showing a fusion of Christian tradition with
Congolese music. Script provides general introduction and comments.

Miriam Makeba

Miriam Makeba

Record, RCA, 1960, $3.98.
Popular treatment of predominantly South African folk songs.

McGraw-Hill

Modern East African Wood Carver

16mm, color, 8 minutes. McGraw-Hill.

A glimpse into the life and work of a modern Makonde wood carver who works in Dar es Salaam. Focus is on a number of his ebony carvings made for eventual sale to Westerners and on his thoughts about his work. Film shows how the tourist trade has changed traditional art. Film suggests that racial, cultural, and social stereotypes about Africans are perpetuated through the tourist demand for pseudo-art.

NET
Duro Ladipo
16mm, b&w, 30 minutes. Indiana, $5.40.

Introduces Duro Ladipo, the founder, director, playwright, composer, and principal male actor of the Duro Ladipo Traveling Theatre Company of Oshogbo, Nigeria. Explains how Ladipo became interested in drama and music. Shows members of the company touring Nigerian villages.

Newmark International Inc. (for Standard Oil) and Modern Talking Picture Service, Inc.
Nigeria: Culture in Transition
16mm, 60 minutes, 1962. Modern Talking Picture Service, Inc., 1212 Avenue of the Americas, New York, N.Y. 10036, free.

Examples of Nigerian culture such as the Mbari House, poetry, the Agbor Dancers, Bugeruab craftsmen, a selection from *The Palm Wine Drinkard* by Amos Tutuola, and a folk opera. The second half consists of a performance of Wole Soyinka's play *The Strong Breed,* (parts of the play have been cut). A teachers guide is available for the film.

Michael Olatunji
Olatunji High Life
Record, script. Columbia, $4.98.

The term "high life" refers to the popular music and dance which developed in Ghana and Nigeria seventy years ago. Album provides samples of "high life" music. Script contains a general discussion of music. No notes on individual bands.

OCA
Music Malawi
Record, script, 1962. OCA, $3.00.

Music recorded at a secondary school in Malawi. Songs are primarily nationalistic. Script notes on individual bands.

Soyinka, Wole (RTV International, producers)
The Swamp Dwellers
16mm, b&w, 46 minutes, 1966. RTV, rental $50.00.

Morgenthau writes: "An important comment on a dominant theme in African writing: the urbanization and modernization of village people." The parents are confirmed traditionalists, seeing the city as a place where everyone gets rich but fearing it at the same time. The son, just returned from the city to look after the crops, rejects the village, returns to the modern city, and finally becomes disillusioned with both.

Efua Sutherland (Leon B. Glickman, producer)
Ababa: The Village Story
16mm, color, 12½ minutes, 1967. For information, write to Mr. Sam Antar, ABC-TV News, 7 West 66th Street, New York, N.Y. 10019.
> Morgenthau writes: "Dramatic material simply and effectively used in the natural setting of a Ghanaian village." A child's view of her village and family that uses some highly stylized movements and poetic language.

U.N. International Zone Series (McGraw-Hill and CON)
In Search of Myself
16mm, b&w, 28 minutes, 1965. CON, rental $8.00, purchase $130.00
> Nigerian life and culture are examined in this film, which reveals the search for identity in Nigerian daily life. Discussion with artists at the Mbari Art Center. Glimpses of Nigeria's contemporary art, music, and literature.

UNESCO, Alexandru Sahia Studios (Bucharest) and Romanian National Commission for UNESCO
First World Festival of Negro Arts, Dakar, 1966
16mm, color, 20 minutes, 1966. UNOPI, rental $8.50, purchase $180.00.
> Impressions of the First World Festival of Negro Arts, Dakar, 1966. Music, dance, sculpture, painting—the reciprocal influence of Negro art and culture in relation to the modern Western world.

UNOPI and CON
African Dances
16mm, color, 28 minutes, 1967. Indiana, CON.
> In the General Assembly Hall at U.N. Headquarters, the Government of Guinea presents *Les Ballets Africains.* The vivacity of this dance group is complemented by the use of traditional instruments.

WTE
The Guitars of Africa (No. 131)
Tape, 22 minutes. WTE, $2.75.
> Discussion of the introduction and spread of the guitar in Africa and the variation caused by local influences. Examples of African calypso and varied styles which have developed. Selections from Uganda, Kenya, and South Africa.

94. *Africa and Afro-American Identity*

Grove Press
Malcolm X: Struggle for Freedom
16mm, 22 minutes, 1964 (before his assassination). Grove Press, rental $22.50, purchase $150.00.

Film centers around Malcolm X responding to questions posed by a narrator. His views as they had evolved toward the end of his life are here
recorded. Some newsreel footage of American civil-rights demonstrations
and new film clips on the South African scene supply the pictorial background for the discussions. For most of the film Malcolm X is on the screen.

John Williams, produced by NET (Bruce Howard and Arthur Rabin)
Omowale — The Child Returns Home
16mm, b&w, sound, 30 minutes, 1965. Indiana, rental $5.40, purchase
$125.00.
Henry Morgenthau writes: "A self-narrated sketch of Williams' search of his
ancestral roots. The return was a disappointment." According to Williams:
"Once you understand your roots . . . you really have no reason to go home
again — especially to one seven generations removed from you." James Mer-
edith, Chinua Archbe, and Cyprian Ekwensi concur. The latter discusses
his own misconceptions of the black man in America. Excellent film for
college level.

100. Research Frontiers in Africa

Ruth Schachter Morgenthau
Separating Spies from Scholars
16mm, 1966. Indiana.
A film talk by Professor Ruth S. Morgenthau of Brandeis University prepared for the African Studies Association Conference, Bloomington, Indiana, October, 1966.

AUDIOVISUAL DISTRIBUTORS: ADDRESSES AND ABBREVIATIONS

AF
African Filmstrips
51 East 42d Street
New York, N.Y. 10017

AMIE
AMIE Associates, Inc.
123 Manhattan Avenue
New York, N.Y. 10025

Atlantis
Atlantis Productions, Inc.
894 Sheffield Place
Thousand Oaks, California 91360

BF
Bailey Films, Inc.

6509 DeLongpre Avenue
Hollywood, California 90028

BIR
Birad Corporation
1564 Broadway
New York, N.Y. 10036

Brandon
Brandon Films, Inc.
200 W. 57th Street
New York, N.Y. 10036

CAFM
Cathedral Films, Inc.
2921 West Alameda Avenue
Burbank, California 91505

CBC
Canadian Broadcasting Corporation
Director of Films
Mr. Don Lytle
1500 Bronson Avenue
Ottawa, Ontario, Canada

CAF
Current Affairs Films
Division of Key Productions, Inc.
527 Madison Avenue
New York, N.Y. 10022

CG
Common Ground Filmstrips
Carman Educational Associates, Inc.
Box 205
Youngstown, N.Y. 14174

Columbia
Columbia Records
Educational Department Orders Service
1400 Fruitridge Avenue
Terre Haute, Indiana 47805

CON
Contemporary Films
245 Park Avenue
New York, N.Y. 10017

Coronet
Coronet Films
488 Madison Avenue
New York, N.Y. 10022

Denoyer-Geppert Co.
5235 Ravenswood Avenue
Chicago, Illinois 60640

DIC
Doubleday
International Communication Films
 Division
Garden City, Long Island, N.Y. 11530

DKB
Desi Kegl-Bognar

221 East 37th Street
New York, N.Y. 10016

EBF
Encyclopedia Britannica Films
4420 Oakton Street
Skokie, Illinois 60076

EFE
Educational Film Enterprises, Inc.
6770 Hollywood Boulevard
Hollywood, California 90028

EG
Eye Gate House, Inc.
146-01 Archer Avenue
Jamaica, N.Y. 11435

Fleetwood Films
10 Fiske Place
Mt. Vernon, N.Y. 10550

FMGM
Free Methodist Church
General Missionary Board
Winona Lake, Indiana 46590

Folkways
Folkways/Scholastic Records
50 West 44th Street
New York, N.Y. 10036

Ghana
Ghana Information Services
Chief of Information
565 Fifth Avenue
New York, N.Y. 10017

Grove Press, Inc.
80 University Place
New York N.Y. 10003

Hayden
Hayden Book Company, Inc.
116 West 14th Street
New York, N.Y. 10011

Mrs. M. J. Herskovits
810 Clinton
Evanston, Illinois 60202

Hoefler
Paul Hoefler Productions
7445 Girard Avenue
Box 1313
La Jolla, California 92037

ICF
International Communication Films
1371 Reynolds Avenue
Santa Ana, California 92705

Illinois
University of Illinois
Visual Aids Service
Champaign, Illinois 61820

Indiana
Indiana University
Audio-Visual Center
Bloomington, Indiana 47402

Jackdaw
Social Studies School Service
4455 Lenox Avenue
Inglewood, California 90304

McGraw-Hill
McGraw-Hill Book Company
Text Film Division
330 West 42d Street
New York, N.Y. 10036

MES
Museum Extension Service
83 Adams Street
Bedford Hills, N.Y. 10507

Methodist Publishing House
A-V Department, Sales Division
201 Eighth Avenue South
Nashville, Tennessee 37203

National Council of Churches
475 Riverside Drive
New York, N.Y. 10027

NET
National Educational Television Film
  Service

Audio-Visual Center
Indiana University
Bloomington, Indiana 47402

Newsweek
Newsweek Educational Division
444 Madison Avenue
New York, N.Y. 10022

NF
Norwood Films
926 New Jersey Avenue, NW
Washington, D.C.

Nystrom
A. J. Nystrom & Company
3333 Elston Avenue
Chicago, Illinois 60618

NYU
New York University Film Library
26 Washington Place
New York, N.Y. 10003

OCA
Operation Crossroads Africa
150 Fifth Avenue
New York, N.Y. 10011

Penn State
The Pennsylvania State University
University Park, Pa.

Philips
Philips Record Co.
35 East Wacker Drive
Chicago, Illinois 60601

RCA
Radio Corporation of America
RCA Educational Services
Camden, N.J. 08108

Robeck
Peter Robeck & Company
230 Park Avenue
New York, N.Y. 10017

RTV International

405 Park Avenue
New York, N.Y. 10028

Shell BP
Shell BP Petroleum Development
  Company of Nigeria, Ltd.
Lagos, Nigeria

Silhouettes
Silhouettes in Courage, Inc.
22 East 40th Street
New York, N.Y. 10016

SVE
Society for Visual Education, Inc.
1345 West Diversey Parkway
Chicago, Illinois 60614

Thorne
Thorne Films, Inc.
1229 University Avenue
Boulder, Colorado 80302

UCOL
University of Colorado
Bureau of Audiovisual Instruction
Attn: Booking Clerk
Boulder, Colorado 80302

UNOPI
United Nations Office of Public In-
  formation
United Nations Plaza
New York, N.Y. 10017

UU
University of Utah
Audiovisual Bureau
Milton Bennion Hall 207
Salt Lake City, Utah 84112

UTP
University Tutorial Press, Ltd.
Clifton House, Euston Road
London, NW1, England

UWF
United World Films, Inc.
221 Park Avenue South
New York, N.Y. 10003

VEC
Visual Education Consultants, Inc.
2840 Laura Lane
Middleton, Wisconsin 53562

WSP
Warren Schloat Production, Inc.
115 Tomkins Avenue
Pleasantville, N.Y. 10570

World
The World Publishing Co.
2231 West 110th Street
Cleveland, Ohio 44102

WTE
World Tapes for Education
P.O. Box 15703
Dallas, Texas 75215

6

Computers
and Africana Bibliographies

KENNETH E. LARIMORE
and DONALD DILLAMAN

MANY ASPECTS OF AFRICAN STUDIES make it an ideal area for experimenting with computerization of bibliographic compilation, storage, retrieval, and print-out. First, the amount of literature is increasing at an extremely rapid rate. As each of the forty-two independent states in Africa develops its own university system, the number of academic journals will probably proliferate even more rapidly than at present. Also, the amount of internationally published materials on Africa has increased significantly in the past few years. Thus, existing bibliographies tend to become out of date within a year or so of their publication. Computerized bibliographies can be brought up to date merely by adding new references to an existing body of references and then producing a new, fully integrated print-out of the entire updated product.

Second, and related to the above, much of the contemporary Africana literature is in the form of journal articles or chapters in anthologies, rather than complete books by single authors. Such references are not usually found in library catalogues or in many of the published bibliographies. A computerized bibliography, by having the capacity for large numbers of references, can accommodate the enormous increase in volume which results from including articles and chapters as well as books.

Third, computerized bibliographies are in aid in *comparative* African studies, which are beginning to increase in importance. One can, for example, collectively retrieve materials on particular ethnic groups, or urban centers, or elites, or political parties, or any other unit (or topic) of analysis, thereby generating a specialized bibliography which meets individual requirements.

Fourth, a computerized bibliography can be an aid to cross-referencing materials. A single bibliographic entry may be retrieved in a number of ways: by author, by date of publication, alphabetically by title, by topic, by keywords in the title, by geographical focus, by type of reference, etc. In cases such as the bibliography in this volume, where topic categories (modules) are used as the basis of organizing a bibliography, a change (e.g., deletion, addition, or modification) by the bibliographer in the categories he has selected may be programmed without difficulty. In short, the organizing categories are not assumed to be permanent, but rather a reflection of needs and perspectives at a particular point in time.

Fifth, from the teacher's point of view, there is a need for up-to-date bibliographies which can be distributed in class. Computer print-out can be adapted to this need in several ways. The simplest way is to make a ditto master either directly, by putting the blank ditto master behind the print-out paper, or indirectly, by making a spirit master from the computer print-out. If inexpensive xerox facilities are available, the print-out may be xeroxed directly on 8½-x-11-inch paper. (In most programs, the references are on the left-hand side of the oversized print-out paper and a series of identification numbers are on the right-hand side. Xeroxing the references on standard-sized paper would eliminate the identification numbers, but these are superfluous for teaching purposes.) In some cases, teachers may want to photo-offset the computer print-out.

Sixth, bibliographies can be individualized in terms of particular university library systems. Thus, for the bibliography in this volume we added a Number Six card, which gives the Northwestern University Library call-numbers for all references. We programmed this call-number *not* to appear in the published version of the bibliography, but we have made available to the Northwestern Library another copy of the bibliography in which it does appear. Any university with computer facilities could take a basic bibliographic computer-tape and program the insertion of a "class of cards" (e.g., Number Six, if using the format of this bibliography) which would give the local call-numbers. A master copy could then be made available for reference at the library.

Seventh, it is as easy to generate computerized bibliographies as *typed* bibliographies. The amount of time required for either typing or key-punching the original references is about the same. In the case of the computerized bibliography, the basic program is already publicly available (i.e., "canned") and hence does not require elaborate programming. Running the final program takes little time. The advantage of computerized bibliographies over typed bibliographies, as mentioned earlier, is primarily in the updating process. Once the basic bibliography has been generated, the other advantages then become available.

COMPUTERS AND REFERENCE RETRIEVAL

The development of electronic computers has made an enormous impact on academic research.[1] The modern computer's ability to store and process large

1. For a good introduction to applications of computer technology in the social sciences see Kenneth Janda, *Data Processing*, 2d ed. (Evanston, Ill.: Northwestern University Press, 1969).

amounts of data allows researchers to deal with problems in hours or days that formerly would have required weeks and months, or even years. Computers are not limited to storing and processing only quantified kinds of information: data in the form of "natural language" are also amenable to computer technology. It is the capability of computers to handle natural language that has led to the development of document retrieval systems,[2] one form of which is computerized bibliographies.

A computerized bibliographic system includes such functions as query formulation, file maintenance, and indexing and delivery of search products. Query formulation is the way in which a user asks the computer to search the bibliography for references. Search commands can be directed towards finding references by particular authors, titles, and subjects. The particular kind of query formulation discussed here involves the use of keywords. Keywords may be specified words or combinations of related words. A user indicates to the computer what constitutes a keyword by either preparing a list of keywords in advance and then submitting them to the computer or by preparing a list of words that are not to be considered keywords.[3] In the first case the computer compares the list of keywords with the information in every bibliographic entry in the collection. When entries are located that contain one or more of these keywords, those entries are prepared for indexing. In the second case, the computer indexes all entries on those words that do not appear in the word list. Most computerized bibliographic systems are so constructed that, if the user desires, only author's names, titles, descriptors, or annotations are searched.

File maintenance is the process of maintaining a relevant bibliographic collection. Publications are put into the collection in a particular way. Most systems involve putting information about an entry on different classes or levels of cards. For example, there may be one class for authors, another for titles, a third for publishing information, and so on. There is usually no limit on the number of cards that may be included within a particular level. If the bibliography is stored on cards, it is a simple matter to physically add new entries and pull out or delete old ones. When the collection is stored on magnetic tape a new entry is punched onto cards and the computer is instructed to add it to the file. Old or undesirable entries are removed from the file by indicating to the computer which entries are to be deleted.

Two systems of indexing and the delivery of search products will be discussed here. Both involve an automatic method for presenting alphabetized listings of keywords contained in the search command. KWIC (Keyword In Context) is a program that arranges keywords in an alphabetized column

---

2. For a good review of the literature on document retrieval see Lawrence H. Berul, "Document Retrieval," in *Annual Review of Information Science and Technology,* ed. Carlos A. Cuadra (Chicago: Encyclopaedia Britannica, 1969), IV, 203-28.

3. Kenneth Janda, *Information Retrieval* (Indianapolis: Bobbs-Merrill, 1968).

surrounded by a few words of the context in which the keyword appear. Figure 1 is an example of information presented in the KWIC format.[4]

FIGURE 1

SAMPLE OF KEYWORD-IN-CONTEXT (KWIC)

SECTION I: KEYWORD LISTING

Title of Article / KEYWORD	Author	Year of Pubn.	Ident. Number
GREECE ABANDONS PROPORTIONAL REPRESENTATION.=	POLYZO AT29		961
BOARDS AND COMMISSIONS CREATED AND ABOLISHED IN 1913.= STATE OFFICERS,	BATES FG14		292
THE MONROE DOCTRINE ABROAD IN 1823–24.=	ROBERT WS12		225
JUDICIAL ABROGATION OF COUNTY HOME RULE IN OHIO.=	SHOUP EL36		1343
ABSENT – VOTING IN NORWAY.=	SABY RS18		474
MILITARY ABSENT – VOTING LAWS.=	RAY PO18		481
ABSENT – VOTING LAWS, 1917.=	RAY PO18		468
ABSENT – VOTING LEGISLATION, 1924–1925.=	RAY PO26		1910
ABSENT VOTERS (LEGISLATION).=	RAY PO14		294
ABSENT VOTING (LEGISLATION).=	LAPP JA16		374
ABSENT VOTING LAWS.=	RAY PO24		702
ABSENT VOTING.=	KETTLE C 17		426
ABSENTEE VOTING IN THE UNITED STATES.=	STEINB PG38		1456
D POLITICS.= ABSOLUTISM AND RELATIVISM IN PHILOSOPHY AN	KELSEN H 48		1941
RELATIVISM, ABSOLUTISM, AND DEMOCRACY.=	OPPENH F 50		2049
Y– THE NATIONAL INTEREST VS. MORAL ABSTRACTIONS.= THE MAINSPRINGS OF AMERICAN	MORGEN HJ50		2039
SOCIAL SCIENCE ABSTRACTS– AN INSTITUTION IN THE MAKING.=	CHAPIN FS30		1035
ON OF CASE STUDIES– THE PROBLEM OF ABUNDANCE (PUBLIC ADMINISTRATION).= PREP	STEIN H 51		2071
PREME COURT DECISIONS– THE USE AND ABUSE OF QUANTITATIVE METHODS.= THE MATHEM	FISHER FM58		2389
GENERAL REPORT OF THE COMMITTEE ON ACADEMIC FREEDOM AND ACADEMIC TENURE.=	AAUP 16		432
RY REPORT OF THE JOINT COMMITTEE ON ACADEMIC FREEDOM AND ACADEMIC TENURE.= PRE	SELIGM ER15		339
T COMMITTEE ON ACADEMIC FREEDOM AND ACADEMIC TENURE.= PRELIMINARY REPORT OF TH	SELIGM ER15		339
E COMMITTEE ON ACADEMIC FREEDOM AND ACADEMIC TENURE.= GENERAL REPORT OF TH	AAUP 16		432
EPORTS OF OCCUPATIONAL DISEASES AND ACCIDENTS (LEGISLATION).= R	ANDREW JB12		211
L SCHEME FOR CLASSIFYING THE STATES ACCORDING TO DEGREE OF INTER – PARTY COMPE	SCHLES JA55		2287
INDUSTRIES.= THE ACCOUNTABILITY OF THE BRITISH NATIONALIZED	JOHNSO EL54		2213
TS.= UNIFORM PUBLIC ACCOUNTING AND STATE SUPERVISION OF ACCOUN	LAPP JA09		132
REORGANIZATION OF THE GENERAL ACCOUNTING OFFICE.=	MCDIAR J 37		1398
ACCOUNTING AND STATE SUPERVISION OF ACCOUNTS.= UNIFORM PUBLIC	LAPP JA09		132
NCIL.= ACHIEVEMENTS OF THE KANSAS LEGISLATIVE COU	GUILD FH35		1297
ITY OF GOVERNMENT EMPLOYEES (HATCH ACT).= FEDERAL RESTRICTIONS UPON THE POLI	HOWARD LV41		1578
THE INDIAN COUNCILS ACT (BRITISH INDIA.).=	SHEPAR WJ09		156
THE MUNICIPAL BANKRUPTCY ACT (SUMNERS – WILCOX BILL).=	SHANKS S 34		1260
EMPLOYEES.= THE HATCH ACT DECISIONS (CAMPAIGNING BY GOVERNMENT	HEADY F 47		1886
– AN INTERPRETATION OF 'KING LEAR,' ACT I, SCENE I.= THE LIMITS OF POLITICS–	JAFFA HV57		2347
THE TRADE AGREEMENT ACT IN COURT AND IN CONGRESS (TARIFF).=	LARKIN JD37		1397
REPEAL OF THE JUDICIARY ACT OF 1801.=	CARPEN WS15		346
OLD AGE PENSIONS– ENGLISH ACT OF 1908.=	SECRIS H 09		124
OLD AGE PENSIONS– FRENCH ACT OF 1910.=	PERKIN C 10		192
THE PARLIAMENT ACT OF 1911, I AND 11.=	DENNIS AL12		206
H CIVIL SERVICE AND THE TRADE UNION ACT OF 1927.= THE BRITIS	MACRAE JH29		978
THE BRITISH TRADE DISPUTES ACT OF 1927.=	MASON AT28		888
THE TRADE DISPUTES AND TRADE UNION ACT OF 1927.= BRITISH TRADE UNION LAW SINC	WITTE EE32		1115
BJECTOR UNDER THE SELECTIVE SERVICE ACT OF 1940.= TREATMENT OF THE CONSCIENTIO	MASLAN JW42		1633
THE FEDERAL REVENUE ACT OF 1942.=	BLAKEY RG42		1650
THE GOVERNMENT CORPORATION CONTROL ACT OF 1945.=	PRITCH CH46		1827
N OF THE LEGISLATIVE REORGANIZATION ACT OF 1946.= THE OPERATIO	GALLOW GB51		2054
THE NEW PRESIDENTIAL SUCCESSION ACT.=	KALLEN JE47		1893
THE FEDERAL REGULATION OF LOBBYING ACT.=	ZELLER B 48		1918
FUNCTIONS UNDER ITS REORGANIZATION ACT.= HOW CONGRESS	THOMAS ED49		1996
HE FEDERAL ADMINISTRATIVE PROCEDURE ACT.= T	SHERWO FH47		1867
THE LABOR CLAUSES OF THE CLAYTON ACT.=	MASON AT24		713
GERMANY'S NEW CIVIL SERVICE ACT.=	MARX FM37		1411
THE BRITISH NATIONAL INSURANCE ACT.=	SHEPAR WJ12		208
RITISH REPRESENTATION OF THE PEOPLE ACT.= THE B	OGG FA18		484
EMPLOYEES' RETIREMENT ACT– MASSACHUSETTS.=	SHERWO GM11		064
THE CANADIAN BANK ACT, 1913.=	RUTHER GW13		257
UNDING FATHERS– A REFORM CAUCUS IN ACTION (THE CONSTITUTIONAL CONVENTION).=	ROCHE JP61		2538
NTERPERSONAL FREEDOM AND FREEDOM OF ACTION.= I	OPPENH FE55		2257
HE POLITICAL IDEAS OF ENGLISH PARTY ACTIVISTS.= T	ROSE R 62		2565
LEGISLATION).= THE ACTIVITIES AND RESULTS OF CRIME SURVEYS (	PFIFFN JM29		979
THE INCREASED CONTROL OF STATE ACTIVITIES BY THE FEDERAL COURTS.=	SCOTT RB09		049
I AND II.= THE DIRECTION OF SUPPLY ACTIVITIES IN THE WAR DEPARTMENT– AN ADMI	MILLET JO44		1710
UMMER SCHOOLS AND OTHER EDUCATIONAL ACTIVITIES OF BRITISH SOCIALIST GROUPS (A	STARR JR36		1361
PROPAGANDA ACTIVITIES OF BRITISH POLITICAL PARTIES.=	STOKE HW36		1325
UMMER SCHOOLS AND OTHER EDUCATIONAL ACTIVITIES OF THE BRITISH LIBERAL PARTY.=	STARR JR37		1406
UMMER SCHOOLS AND OTHER EDUCATIONAL ACTIVITIES OF THE BRITISH CONSERVATIVE PAR	STARR JR39		1495
TING TURNOUT).= ACTIVITIES OF THE COLORADO ELECTORATE (VO	SPENCE RC23		663
STUDY OF COMMITTEES).= LEGISLATIVE ACTIVITY IN MASSACHUSETTS, 1916 (STATISTI	HAINES WH17		440
ION).= POLITICAL ACTIVITY OF AMERICAN CITIZENS (PARTICIPAT	WOODWA JL50		2041
RAL RESTRICTIONS UPON THE POLITICAL ACTIVITY OF GOVERNMENT EMPLOYEES (HATCH A	HOWARD LV41		1578
L OF ADMINISTRATIVE AND LEGISLATIVE ACTS IN FRANCE.= JUDICIAL CONTRO	GARNER JW15		355
JUDICIAL REVIEW OF LEGISLATIVE ACTS IN GERMANY.=	BLACHL FF27		842
MUNICIPAL LEGALIZING ACTS IN IOWA (LEGISLATIVE STATISTICS).=	SCHAFF O 32		1130
NEW PRIMARY AND CORRUPT PRACTICES ACTS IN MINNESOTA.=	SCHAPE WA13		235
STITUTIONAL AMENDMENTS AND REFERRED ACTS, NOVEMBER ELECTION, 1914.= CON	BATES FG15		318
THE POLITICAL PHILOSOPHY OF HENRY ADAMS.=	SHUMAT RV34		1234
HE LIMITS OF SOCIAL SCIENCE– HENRY ADAMS' QUEST FOR ORDER (POLITICAL THOUGHT	KARIEL H 56		2325
IONAL THEORIES AND PRINCIPLES.= THE ADAPTATION OF ADMINISTRATIVE LAW AND PROCE	HAINES CG40		1508
AND TENDENCIES (APSA PRESIDENTIAL ADDRESS) POLITICAL DEVELOPMENTS	FAIRLI JA30		985

4. This data was taken from Kenneth Janda, ed., *Cumulative Index to the American Political Science Review, Volumes 1–57, 1906–1963* (Evanston, Ill.: Northwestern University Press, 1964).

KWOC (Keyword Out of Context) indexing involves printing the alphabetized keywords in a separate column alongside the original context, as shown in Figure 2.[5]

FIGURE 2

SAMPLE OF KEYWORD-IN-CONTEXT (KWOC)

898   Koinage–Kreinin

```
    KOINAGE MBIYU
    THE PEOPLE OF KENYA SPEAK FOR THEMSELVES.
    DETROIT, KENYA PUBLICATION FUND, 1955
    055,117-06,

KOMAROVSKY MIRRA
    KOMAROVSKY MIRRA
    THE VOLUNTARY ASSOCIATIONS OF URBAN DWELLERS.
    AMERICAN SOCIOLOGICAL REVIEW 11 DECEMBER 1946 PP 686-698
    (BOBBS-MERRILL REPRINT 151)
    046,

KOPF DAVID
    KOPF DAVID          VON DER MUHLL G
    POLITICAL SOCIALIZATION IN KENYA AND TANZANIA.
    JOURNAL OF MODERN AFRICAN STUDIES 5 MAY 1967 PP 13-51
    043,117-03,136-03,

KOPYTOFF IGOR
    KOPYTOFF IGOR
    CLASSIFICATION OF RELIGIOUS MOVEMENTS-ANALYTICAL AND
    SYNTHETIC
    IN SYMPOSIUM ON NEW APPROACHES TO THE STUDY OF RELIGION,
    PROCEEDINGS OF THE 1964 ANNUAL SPRING MEETING OF THE
    AMERICAN ETHNOLOGICAL SOCIETY,SEATTLE 1964 PP 77-90
    051,

    KOPYTOFF IGOR
    EXTENSION OF CONFLICT AS A METHOD OF CONFLICT RESOLUTION
    AMONG THE SUKU OF THE CONGO.
    JOURNAL OF CONFLICT RESOLUTION 5 MARCH 1961, PP 61-69
    057,108-01,

KOTSCHAP V
    HANCE WILLIAM A       KOTSCHAP V         PETEREC RICHARD J
    SOURCE AREAS OF EXPORT PRODUCTION IN TROPICAL AFRICA.
    GEOGRAPHIC REVIEW 51 OCTOBER 1961 PP 487-499
    069,

KOUBETTI V
    RAMIN JEAN CHARLES  KOUBETTI V          GUILHEM MARCEL
    HISTOIRE DU DAHOMEY.
    PARIS, L'AFRIQUE-LE MONDE, COURS MOYEN, LIGEL, 1964
    109-02,

KRADER LAWRENCE
    KRADER LAWRENCE
    THE FORMATION OF THE STATE.
    ENGLEWOOD CLIFFS, NEW JERSEY, PRENTICE-HALL, 1968
    006,009,

KRAUS  JON
    KRAUS  JON
    ARMS AND POLITICS IN GHANA
    IN CLAUDE WELCH (ED), SOLDIER AND STATE IN AFRICA, EVANSTON
    NORTHWESTERN UNIVERSITY PRESS, 1970
    064,

KREININ
    KREININ MORDECHAI E
```

5. Data from *The African Experience Volume IIIA: Bibliography.*

The advantage of KWIC is that because only one line per entry is printed, there is economy of space. KWOC, on the other hand, prints the complete citation (if desired) with each entry.[6] KWOC, therefore, is probably a better system for bibliographies.

Although computers accept information from a variety of media (e.g., punched cards, magnetic tape, printed matter), most bibliographic collections intended for the computer are first put on punch cards in natural language and then transferred to magnetic tape. The tape stores the card images in a smaller amount of space. A typical magnetic tape can store about 120 boxes of cards. Hence, the costs of handling and distributing the bibliography are lessened.

The disadvantage of computerized bibliographic systems is that they demand ready access to computing equipment. Universities that have their own computing centers with sufficient hardware have little difficulty in installing computerized bibliographies. Universities and colleges without their own computing center but with a terminal and access capabilities can also easily incorporate computerized bibliographies to meet their needs. Remote processing involves a central computer capable of storing and processing data. To this central computer, universities, colleges, and, increasingly, departments are connected by remote terminals. Terminals permit the transfer of input commands to the computer and the transfer of output back to the user at the remote terminal. In such a system the bibliographic information would be stored at the central computer site. A user at a remote terminal would relay to the computer the kind of bibliographic references he wants and the computer would relay that information back to the user via the terminal. If the remote terminal does not have the facility for high-speed printing the information could be printed at the central site and delivered to the user by some other means.

THE AFRICAN EXPERIENCE BIBLIOGRAPHY

The KWOC format was chosen for the bibliography of *The African Experience*. This format has been followed, however, more for the sake of compiling future bibliographies than for the sake of easing the preparation of this volume. With the rapid increase of publications on Africa, it has seemed imperative to be able to generate up-to-date bibliographies without having to reprocess manually all the previous references. This can be done using KWOC computer retrieval and print-out. Deletions may also be made as new works replace older works. In the preparation of this volume alone, over 1,500

6. Janda discusses the relative merits of KWOC and KWIC in *Data Processing*, especially pages 190–202.

key-punched references were excluded from the final print-out because the authors felt they had become redundant in the course of the time taken to prepare this bibliography.

Apart from the ease of amendments and reproduction of future bibliographies there are other advantages to the KWOC format. Keywords, such as names of ethnic groups, countries, and substantive themes, may be used to retrieve entries. The actual card format is quite simple. On the first card level of each entry the author's name appears; on the second card level is the title of the work; on the third card level the publishing information appears. In this bibliography the fourth card level has been used for the "descriptor," which is the module number in the *Syllabus;* and the fifth card level is used for annotation purposes. This is illustrated in Figure 3.

FIGURE 3
KEY TO BIBLIOGRAPHIC CARDS

Description	Sample	Card Numbers
Name	Bohannan, Paul	1.1
Book Title	Africa and Africans	2.1
Publisher	New York Natural History Press 1964	3.1
Descriptor (module number)	01	4.1
Annotation	Successful attempt to put African culture in	5.1
	modern perspective. Informal, personal state-	5.2
	ment by outstanding anthropologist, which is	5.3
	challenging and often controversial. Covers wide	5.4
	range from early peopling of continent, to nation-	5.5
	alism and independence. Examines early state for-	5.6
	mation, the slave trade, colonialism, the arts,	5.7
	family life, economy, religion. Basic introduc-	5.8
	tory reading.	5.9
Name	Fagan, Brian M.	1.1
Article Title	The Iron Age Sequence in the Southern Province	2.1
	of Northern Rhodesia	2.2
Journal	Journal of African History 4 1963 pp. 157-77	3.1
Descriptor (module number)	18	4.1
Annotation	Case Study	5.1

TECHNICAL ASPECTS OF COMPUTERIZED BIBLIOGRAPHIES

In this section, a discussion of the more technical aspects of the retrieval system used in this bibliography will be attempted. This discussion will be based on how the retrieval system works at the Vogelback Computing Center, Northwestern University, on a CDC 6400 computer. The intention is to explain the system in enough detail so that persons in other universities and colleges can make a decision as to whether or not it might be feasible to incorporate this bibliography and Northwestern's retrieval system into their own computing facilities. At the Northwestern computing center KWOC is only one part of TRIAL, which is

> an information processing system that will perform editing, indexing, and retrieval of textual and certain types of numeric information. The system allows for the creation and maintenance of a master file (EDIT), indexing on words designated as "key" words or, alternatively, on every word in the text, excluding those common terms that are user supplied as "stop" word list (INDEX), and computer retrieval and printout of entries that satisfy a user search command (SEARCH). The system is designed such that any one or any combination of the above features can be achieved through one computer run with proper control cards.[7]

The TRIAL package includes KWOC, KWIC, and a search phase that has been used for SDI (Selective Dissemination of Information), a bibliographic service available to faculty and students at Northwestern. The TRIAL system is written in FORTRAN, using approximately 4,000 source cards, and is designed to be user-oriented. There is an on-line version of the SEARCH phase that permits the user to interact with the computer while the program is operating. The TRIAL file-structure allows for a maximum of nine levels or classes of information for each bibliographic entry (of which only 5 have been used in this published bibliography). The system also permits entries in the file to be added to, deleted, replaced, and altered. Finally, the TRIAL program in conjunction with INDEX includes a STATISTICS option "available for counting and printing the total number of occurrences in a file of a key or stop word; the FREQUENCY option will print a listing of all words and their frequency within a given entry which will be used as indexing terms in KWOC output."[8] The core storage necessary for this program is 25,000 computer words on the CDC 6400; each computer word can contain ten characters. The cost of the TRIAL system is nominal for the output produced. On a bibliography of about 3,800 entries, the KWOC program has searched, sorted, and

7. Lorraine Borman and Donald Dillaman, *TRIAL: Users Manual* (Vogelback Computing Center, Northwestern University, October, 1968, rev. December 1968, NUCC118), p. 1.

8. *Ibid.,* p. 36.

printed-out the complete information for all entries by author in an alphabetized list for a cost of about $50.

Any computing center using a CDC computer would have little difficulty
implementing the TRIAL program at their installation. There is also available
through the Northwestern computing center, however, a version of TRIAL
adapted to the IBM 360-series computers. The IBM 360 version requires tape
drives, disk packs, and the standard IBM sort-merge package. Copies of the
TRIAL program, not including the on-line SEARCH, are available upon
request from Vogelback Computing Center to other computing centers but
not, as a general rule, to individuals. The computing center requesting the
program must provide a tape and pay nominal costs involved in processing.
The cost to nonprofit institutions is lower than the charge to other kinds of
organizations.

Correspondence or queries may be addressed to Vogelback Computing
Center, Northwestern University, Evanston, Illinois 60201.

The Contributors

ROBERT PLANT ARMSTRONG is Director of Northwestern University Press and has traveled extensively in Africa.

WILLIAM G. BYRNE is engaged in graduate studies at the School of Education, Northwestern University, and has taught for several years at Chicago City College.

DONALD DILLAMAN is completing his graduate studies in mathematics at Northwestern University; he is a research associate at Vogelback Computing Center.

AHMAD GETSO is an instructor in Hausa at Northwestern University; he is from Kano, Nigeria.

MORRIS GOODMAN is Associate Professor of Linguistics at Northwestern University and has taught both Hausa and Swahili.

ROBERT KOESTER is Assistant Librarian of Africana, Northwestern University; he served in the Peace Corps in Nigeria.

KENNETH E. LARIMORE is completing his graduate studies in political science at Northwestern University; he was in the Peace Corps in Guinea.

JOSEPH MABWA is an instructor in Swahili at Northwestern University; he is originally from Kenya.

JOHN N. PADEN is Assistant Professor of Political Science at Northwestern University; a former Rhodes scholar, he is the author of the forthcoming *Religion and Political Culture in Northern Nigeria*.

HANS E. PANOFSKY is Curator of Africana, Northwestern University Library, and has traveled extensively in Africa.

EDWARD W. SOJA is Associate Professor of Geography at Northwestern University and has taught at the University of Ibadan in Nigeria; he is the author of *The Geography of Modernization in Kenya*.